Dear Diane

I hope you

of:

Poems from the Heart

It's a variety of all topics as
per the cover.

Love,

D. Teresa

Poems from the Heart

Doreen Kovach

To order additional copies of this book, contact:
Xlibris Corporation
1-888-795-4274
www.Xlibris.com
Orders@Xlibris.com
57253

In honor of her parents, Andrew and Gloria Kovach

HERALD THE EMERALD!

They met, courted and married in New York City,
    And Mom found that Dad was very witty.
All through these fifty-five years,
    You've had some happy times and shed some tears.
You joked and were happy, yet sometimes sad,
    But mostly during these years you were glad.
Long time ago Dad met Mom in Manhattan,
    When I look at old photos he was quite a man.
My Mom is unique and dresses to perfection,
    She always tells me she was her mother's reflection.
Both my parents have come through the waters which were rough,
    Dad came out fighting especially tough.
Through darkness through the night and many a plight,
    You've come through seeing the star's light.
Many lives Dad likes to enhance,
    While mom likes to dance.
All through the years you've shown compassion and kindness,
    Not only to people but to animals you caress.
You were frightened by Charlie the peaceful dove,
    But all and all you exalted a lot of love.

        Doreen Teresa Kovach
        May 2, 2009

Contents

Acknowledgements

I would especially like to thank my parents, Andrew and Gloria Kovach for all their support, encouragement and all the fine education I received through the years. I attended St. Michael's here in Palisades Park, NJ; St. Cecilia's in Englewood, NJ; and the College of St. Elizabeth's in Convent Station, NJ.

I'd like to thank my past teachers: 4th grade, English teacher Mrs. O'Connor for encouraging me in the Poetic field after seeing *The Robins* and *O Dear Jesus.* I'd be remiss if I'd didn't mention Sister Marie Harold, S.C. of St. Cecilia's who taught both Poetry and Creative Writing and Sr. Anne Ford S.C. of the College of Saint Elizabeth, Professor Emeritus of Poetry (Eng. & American.) I developed a fondness for certain poets such as Poe, e.e. cummings, Frost, and lest I not forget two of my favorites Gerard Manley Hopkins and Milton.

I'd now like to thank all the people who so diligently worked on typing my poetry and put it in order. My sincerest thanks go to Angela Meglio who spent hours typing and to Joe Klech who put most of the poems on discs. Thanks also to Maria Rendon who also helped put poems on discs.

And finally I give thanks to Miss Jeanne Aimone, my best friend who finalized and reread every poem and proofread everything with me as we embarked on this journey.

To all a Sincere and Profound
Thank you

Doreen Kovach

Definition of Notation

AG—Animal General
AC—Animal Cats
CG—Calendar General
CS—Calendar Seasonal
EG—Emotion General
EH—Emotion Happy
ES—Emotion Sad
M—Miscellaneous
PG—Person General
PF—Person Family
RG—Religious General
RI—Religious Icon
S—Sports
T—Travel
WG—Weather General
WS—Weather Seasonal

THE ROBINS

The Robins again are here in town,
They are back safe and sound.
The Robins are flying here and there,
They are flying everywhere.
The Robins are flying high and low,
They are flying fast and slow.
The men are trying to get to the moon,
While the Robins are singing a lovely tune.
Then in winter they go away,
You see them go day by day.
After winter they return in spring,
You can hear them sing and sing.
In spring comes the ICE—CREAM CART,
But still and all the Robins are very smart.

Age 9
March 1965

O DEAR JESUS

O DEAR JESUS, We all loveYou
You are the one that makes it rain;
You also send the morning dew
You even heal the lame.

O DEAR JESUS, You made everything
All the people, land and seas;
You made the birds sing
And You made the bees.

O DEAR JESUS, OUR BELOVED SAVIOUR
We have hope to go YOUR WAY;
You shall judge us by our behavior
On that very special Judgment Day.

Amen.

Age 11
1967

COLORFUL HINTS

If you like red
You've got a head.
Redhead

If you like green
Go eat a bean!
Greenbean

If you like blue
There's your shoe.
Blue shoes

If you like yellow
Bet you're mellow.
Mellow-yellow

If you like tan
Sunny is your man.
Tan Man

If you like gold
Your cash is cold.
Cold gold

If you like pink
Go to the ice rink.
Pink rink

If you like brown
Go out on the town.
Brown-town

If you like gray
Rainy is your day.
Gray Day

If you like black
Pull a jack.
BLACKJACK!

Age 21
1977

A MOTHER

What is a mother?
She is one who is no other.
She may be young or may be old
But comes from God's pot o gold.
She may live close or far
She's worth a golden star.
She could've worked durin' her life,
Or maybe was just a housewife.
Her temper may be hot
And she may yell a lot.
Or is she very carefree?
Singing from here to eternity.
Instead of talking she may be quiet
Perhaps she cares for a pet.
Maybe she enjoys playing cards
While others prefer to work in their yards.
Whichever type you possess
To each mother, MAY GOD BLESS.

Age 21
May 1977

PARADISE

Olive trees surround me
We are on a blurry path
Into the future.
The future is cloudy,
Only Olive trees visible.
And the winding,
dusty, trail ahead. Yes—
Hills and dales.
But again more olive trees.
Someone inquires:
This is the ride to Paradise?
I calmly reply;
This Now Paradise
is Spain—Spain.
A peace like the moon's
Sea of Tranquillity.
A mystic nature, reaching

Nirvana.

Age 21
June 1977

THANKSGIVING POEM FOR PARENTS

I thank you both
For all you've done.
For everything you finished
That I had begun.

I thank you for all
You've given to me.
For making me realize
What I should be.

I thank you for accepting
My many mistakes.
And thank you for
giving me a break.

Age 22
Nov. 1978

TESSIE AND JOE

T is for Theresa
E is for Easygoing
S is for your career as Seamstress
S is for your Sugar-coating
I is for Independence
E is for Everything.

A is for And many more
N is for so Near
D is for being so Dear.

J is for Joseph
O is for the O.T.B.
E is for the Exacta four-three.

Age 30
Sept. 1986

MY GRANDPARENTS

M is for Mine Only.
Y is for Yours Truly.

G is for your many Good Deeds
R is for Running here and there
A is for being Around to care
N is for fulfilling our many Needs.
D is for being so very Dear
P is for Patience you show
A is for Always on the go
R is for that '86 Ruby year.
E is for Evermore
N is for your Niceties
T is for being Trustworthy
S is f or my love for Sure . . .

Age 30
Sept. 1986

A PAINFUL LESSON

*I looked at the calendar
and what did I see?
October 11th next week
staring at me.*

*I cried so hard
My stomach almost burst,
Thinking of that convent
That of which I thirst.*

*My thoughts are so scrambled
I can't even think,
My heart might as well
be in the kitchen sink.*

*I long for the day
When I finally mature,
It can't be too soon
This is for sure.*

*I must try harder
If this is my desire,
To serve the Lord God
As a "NUN for Hire".*

*I'll be in my glory
When I board that plane,
With a one-way ticket
To my destiny—Spain.*

*I'll teach those children
In northern Mondragon,
Not only of English
Also of God and his Son.*

*Age 31
Oct 4, 1987*

THE WORST DISEASE

I have the worst disease ever
It's called "Foot in the Mouth,"
Many a friendship it'll sever
It chases me north and other south.

So far I know no cure
Of which I can depend,
My problems I still endure
I admit I'm at "Dead End".

Therefore I've got to turn around
And face life's other direction,
Hopefully I'll make a rebound
Using Humility as my Medication.

Patience ain't too bad either
When climbing up the mountain,
For if I choose neither
I should be in the Lion's Den.

A touch of the Bible, a bit of Maria
Wisdom, Guidance and Prayer,
Will get me to Iberia
Hoping it'll be forever.

Age 31
Oct. 1987

THE BEAST

Doctor
Is evil,
A Satan
A Devil
Pain in
the ass.
Here to
hurt us
on this
planet
Earth.
I hated
So many.
Needle
Inject
My body.
I Panic,
Wobble,
Scream
and cry
Shaken
I'll try
again.

Maybe.

Age 33
Nov 1989

Letter

Dentist
on and on
drill me.
Sit back
Thinking
of worst.
I fear of
all in my
mouth. Oh
GAS, GAS
deadens
my being.
Drills a—
gain. Why?
Pain all
in mouth.
Scared I
breathe
listen
to radio.
Soothes
the mind.
Finally
filling
in mouth.

Age 33
Nov. 1989

DOCTORS

Most doctors are not so very nice
In fact, some are as cold as ice.
Dr. Pilar entered at 14, a Queen
She's sweet, kind & nice not mean.
When I was down and out, so discombobulated
With all my pills, got heavily sedated.
In Englewood Hospital met Dr. Napoli,
I tell you he's as sweet as a cannoli.
To alls amazement he called me intelligent
With fondness, I still remember the word Diligent.
Dr. N. said that I was deeply infatuated
Hey, I need all the love I can saturate.
Even got the chance to see Dr. DePirro,
And his love he also did bestow.
Nurses said, "sensitive to needs of another",
Still wish I had a different mother.
When with Dr. N. and Mr. L. called me abash,
Hoooolly—did I ever wanna dash.
It's about three weeks at the hospital
It's like a trip to the Bergen Mall.
Although I seem a lot better
Still wish I were an Irish Setter.
Yes, me and my language recognizance
Just wish I had more common sense.
Also the lack of ability
And surely need emotional stability.

Age 35
July 1991

UNTIMELY LOVE

It was March 15th of '92
When I found my thrill,
Forget about Larry
Say 'Hello' to Bill.

As I stepped from the bus
I saw he was Mr. Right,
He smiled and greeted me
So cute to my delight.

We dined at Corky's Corner
And had a bit of brunch;
He talked, chatted and quipped
While I quietly tried to munch.

I have a female calico cat
While he has a cockatoo,
Yet just like little ole me
He's an only child too.

He then decided to drive me home
But to meet again is his desire,
As we conversed and finally parted
He started to ignite my fire.

Age 35
March 1992

THE MAGIC OF SPAIN

Thinking of the Magic of Spain
Flowing from the flood of sweet serenity.
Even the droplets of soft rain
Pelting the cross backdrop of memories.

One rising after the other
Sweetly, gently, caressing, yet always forever.

Breathtaking toros running through Pamploma
With Gradiosa Granada having Lavish Gardens.
Brandishing beaches of Coastal Barcelona
All people with emotions that never harden.

Celestial high Cathedral per each mayor city
While street performers do their nightly ditty.

El Grecos of Toledo opposing Gran Mystics of Avila
Hidden cave dwelling of Cozy Cuenca.
Palatable paella served up in Valencia
While swaying palms drift in Palencia.

Don Juans and Quijote, El Prado and El Cid
All wrapped up in Capitol Royal Madrid.

Flan, Horchata, and Flamenco served on sidewalk café
Planned for each crystallized Mediterranean day.

Age 38
Aug. 1994

THAT MAGIC MOMENT

St. Patrick's Parade was as sweet as fudge
John Cardinal O'Connor chosen Grand Marshall.
On the corner of 49ᵗʰ, I would not budge
Amidst throngs of people, wall to wall.

I was to go, I vowed
Only to see him—
It was to be a moment so proud
He is still so neat and trim!

The weather displayed quite a breeze
As he strolled with his vigor and vim.
For over two miles, he strode with ease
With clouds passing and casting dim.

He demonstrated a steady gait
And took so much pride
Representing New York City and State
As he took his mighty stride.

When he passed we all screamed, "Hi"!
In between sips of coffee and tea.
We don't wish to bid you "Goodbye"!
On that day so free, so carefree.

He represents the Father, Son
And Spirit, called the Holy Trinity.
All people's hearts forever won
On earth second to Thee.

At seventy five, still very spry
Marching in sixth place as planned.
Let retirement be a big lie
I said when he surprisingly shook my hand.

It was there on street forty-nine
How could I again be the chosen one?
His personality is so very fine
I thanked God for his act well done.

After the handshake, I did cry
He was truly sent from Heaven above.
Cardinal O'Connor is quite a guy
His grip being as tight as a glove.

He worked his way through the crowd
Then taking place on his stand.
Each and every group grew very loud
Interspersed by varied band.

His attitude was very humble
He returned to make a special call.
Blessed a fan who took a stumble
Hoping it was not a serious fall.

God sent us this special dove
To watchers he did please.
We all sent him lots of love
And at times, he threw us a tease.

He is like our Big Brother
A very big Smash Hit.
Surly like no other
Occasionally showing humor and wit.

He represents the Vine
He represents the Spirit.
His health still so fine
Can't retire, can't let him quit.

Age 39
March 1995

A TRIBUTE TO A SPECIAL PERSON

'Tis the year 1995, special day of March 17th
a special day for John Cardinal O'Connor.
Saint Pat's up Fifth, and wearin' of the green
The parades Grand Marshall, what a special honor!

Truly a great day for the Irish
With blessed food of cabbage & corned beef,
Served on Waterford Crystal dish
Glistening beautifully like a coral reef.

His eyes'll truly smile
He's representing the Sede of New York;
Even using Irish Spring, instead of Dial
Knowing it's Friday, he abstains from Pork!

With everyone wearin' a Holy Shamrock
And joyfully singing the Tura, lura, lura;
All's a marchin' in time with Kilts and Socks
To him give three cheers, then "Erin go bragh!"

Long live a very special man
Let your retirement be a wild rumor.
This comes from your avid New Jersey fan
Who doesn't want you to lose your sense of humor.

Age 39
March 1995

SEASONS

Winter—*is drab-gray*
claiming December thru February
sometimes even into March;
with ice-pellets, freezing rain,
slick snow making sidewalks
slippery like an eel.
Initiating accidents on wet
torn roads-pavement broken.
Stores selling shovels,
umbrellas, rubbers and boots.
Sales are brisk until
days grow longer & sun returns,
Something's in the air.

It's called **Spring**—
usually mid-March thru June and with it
Hope springs eternal.
A new season, a new time—
Freshness abounds to all
Green grass, dew drops.
Flower buds approaching
especially purple crocus popping.
Birds chirping and tweeting—
Clocks change, days lengthen,
Moore sunshine and warmth
Sales now brisk for short-shorts
*swimwear and bikinis—bearing skin—***SPRING***.

And just like that at the
Vernal equinox there's—SUMMER.
June, July, and August,
World has turned around
Facing the other direction.
Lots of sun sweeping down
Causing hot, humid, blistery days—
Scorching skin of sleepy beachgoers
Searing soles of boardwalk feet
Scenes of bikes versus cars,
Pushcarts of dogs and burgers
Lots of ice-cream floats and shakes.

But then we stumble,
We fall gently into—AUTUMN.
Boardwalks close down, winds pick-up,
Schools reopen—sales soar on
pens, pencils, pads and backpacks.
Leaves discolor losing
Chlorophyll, falling to earth.
Nights lengthen, days grow short.
Layered clothes reappear, Cardigans
buttoned, shoes replacing
sandals and REEBOKS—
Swimming, baseball, and tennis vanishing
replaced by hockey, skis and sleds.

Age 39
April 1995

IN REMEMBERANCE

Seventy one, two, three and four
The years of the Vietnam War.
It was a task, a lousy chore
Making home emotions very sore
Whence coming home, closing the door
And leaving at most, many poor.

Shouts resounded, "Hell no, we won't go."
To fight this dreaded enemy and ferocious foe
Only to see each GI JOE
Fall down row by row
Or possibly be shot in the toe
So lie down and lay low.

Most shouted, "Two, four, six, eight
Why don't we retaliate?"
Most died meeting up with fate
Some leaving behind a beautiful mate.
Sooner or later we all started to hate
Some finally arrived home safe but late.

Others chanted, "Will Vietnam satisfy the Reds?"
Maybe their intention was to behead
Then let lie and deprive of a bed
Soon to see hundreds or more dead
If not by fire, then by lead
A sight the sane would truly dread.

Lots of protesters fled the draft,
Went to Canada and were laughed
While most above fought by mighty aircraft
And the rest on the seas in a raft.
All left behind his own craft
This being many years after President Taft.

Most bellicose events happened in Hanoi
Accompanied by loss of innocence and joy;
Using real guns instead of the toy
And real man, not the youthful boy
Each eating and using lots of soy
With camouflage being used as a decoy.

Now Hanoi is called Saigon
It is part of Viet Cong.
The Delta was the MeKong
Peace was pierced like a fork prong
Like torched coals on hot tongs.
Especially at the GI's base of Qui Nhom.

Another city was Ho Chi Minh
Ruining calm and creating din.
Soldiers on both sides making sin
Knowing neither could not win,
Sometimes standing as if a piece of tin
While at the barracks, drank their gin.

Each year, troops were visited by Bob Hope
Bringing along cheer so each could cope,
And dispelling myths of being a dope
Blessings even came from the Pope,
While families sent gifts including soap
Any little item, to ease their facial grope.

Bombs then were made of napalm
Thus creating a lot of harm,
Destroying both the Civilian calm
And also to beautiful swaying palm.
While nations recited the psalms
And humble citizens offered alms.

Another tragedy was the AK 47 missile
With the passing sounds so shrill
Certainty did its job—TO KILL.
And not being much of a thrill
Each soldier certainly got his fill
Flying and doing this harmful drill.

Back home, here at Ohio Kent
All youth tried to vent,
All our anger we had pent
Our support we truly lent,
To our boys who were sent
Through some never ever went.

All the accounted dead to a body bag
Each body looking thin and hag.
The clothes resembling pieces of rag,
None of them beforehand did brag
While to top officials we'd nag.
In shame, all tails did wag.

In '75, North and South merged and met
Our men arrived home jet by jet.
Some who were involved in Tet
Soon to be nicknamed, 'Vietnam Vet'.
Each certainly encountered enormous debt
And felt like the hole in a fish net.

Just like that the date is April 30
I don't know where each may be.
I do know those alive are now set free.
Even after many a governmental plea
Thru many a river, many a sea,
The Paris Peace Accord was the key.

And now twenty years later in 1995
Some memories we do revive.
Let's be glad the remainder live.
It is time now that we all strive
To give freedom and not deprive
Let us give 'em all a High-Five.

Age 39
April 1995

DOREEN KOVACH

KITTENS

Newborn little puffs of fluff
Naked as a rubber mouse
Same size too.
Frail and thin
Lacking skin.
Helpless, unable to move
Toothpick like tails,
Tiny triangular shaped ears
Pink noses like pebbled sand,
Slit eyes that won't open
For a few weeks
They are just kittens.

Kittens, helpless, dependent on mom
Sometimes even on a human one,
For they too are babies.
Needing regular two hour feedings
Lots of milk, water and formula
Also TLC and affection.
The unending list goes on
And heaven forbid you don't come thru
They squeak, yelp and give a loud MEW!
"Hay ma-feeding time is near".
And afterwards with a full belly
They acknowledge you with a contented purr
And finally just like a babe they go to sleep.

Age 39
June 1995

BIRTHDAYS

Birthdays are irresponsible
They sneak up on you and
Make you grow older.
People force you to eat and party
Causing indigestion along with
Gray hair sprouting from the roots
And your face attracting wrinkles.
Your joints begin to hurt and ache
Then arthritis sets in and bones are brittle,
Vericose and spider veins set in
Sooner or later you need a cane.
The eyes go and you start to squint—
Some people need glasses or contacts.
Teeth begin to decay and fall out
Most need caps, crowns or dentures.
Some parts of the human corpus begins to sag
Eventually the kidneys go
And one becomes incontinent.
Sooner or later everything goes
And one DIES—so much for
Growing old and BIRTHDAYS.

Age 39
June 1995

THE GREAT LAKES AND NEW YORK

I learned two easy lessons in grammar school
They should be very useful tools.
The lakes are known by the acronym HOMES;
So these should be two simple poems.

H is for the Indian Lake of Huron,
O is for Canada's Lake Ontario,
M is for the shore of Lake Michigan,
E is for the dam connecting Lake Erie,
S is for the largest of 'em all, Lake Superior.

The second lesson, can be learned with ease,
In fact, in a jiffy, like a breeze
It is all New York and about
With various places, sites and its clout.

I like to use the acronym LIMBS of NY

LI is for the largest, thus being Long Island,
M is for the most popular—Manhattan,
B means Broken Line—now Brooklyn,
S is for Staten Island,
NY is obviously for New York City.

These two poems may seem long
But are quite clever,
I know you cannot go wrong
Not once, not twice, not ever.

Age 39
July 1995

MICK, THE QUICK

As a youth growing up in the Sixties
I knew a famed baseball player,
His uniform number was lucky seven
His name was Mantle and he made the grade
And everyone knew him as the Mick.

He played for the New York Yankees
In the grand house that Ruth built,
In the midst of his heyday-being in seventh heaven
Playing Major Leagues for about two decades
He had a magic to make the bat and ball click.

Hitting and slugging consistently came with ease
He easily entered the renowned Hall,
Always getting along with his revered brethren
And never used his illness as facades
But he did play and got the nickname "Quick".

Quick Mick is now '63
He's admitting a lot of his past guilt,
But in his game he was always driven
Whether playing in the Bronx or the Everglades
Even while playing with teammate Michael, the Stick.

His leg and muscle pain were like stinging bees
Also associated with a feeling of wilt,
He always extended himself to play a game so leaven
He truly represented a humanistic yet hellish Hades
While deep down playing smoothly and being slick.

Thirty years later and into the mid nineties
Baseball pros and cons have hit the hilt,
Baseball attitudes need to be more even Steven
The older rules should be laid
Of the lot, Micky Mantle's still my pick.

Age 39
1995

HIS HOLINESS, POPE JOHN PAUL II

We welcome a friend known as Pope John Paul II
And so we pay homage to His Holiness
He always comes greeting fellow Christians and Jews
And on his travels many does he bless.

To many of us he is quite a religious and historic man
Going from site to site with a specific call
Therefore, on each trip, he'll travel in his Papal van
With his followings having a ball.

John Paul is a traditional Pope
Coming from a distant and faraway land
He always offers and delivers hope
Just as originally planned.

Among his flock, He has many a fan
I'll attest that Our Holy Pontiff has a large fold
He attacks each problem with a unique plan
Making him come from a fortuitous mold.

Even when our Holy Father's under duress
He offers the elderly and youth his outstretched hand
Also meeting with various media and press
Which shows he is in complete command.

Religiously His Holiness will be bold
When meeting with friend or foe
Deep down he always has a heart of Gold
Thus giving John Paul's face a caring glow.

Doreen Kovach,
Papal Visit Giant Stadium

Age 39
October 4, 1995

OF HUMAN BONDAGE, WEAKNESS, FRAILTIES I SEARCH WHY

He couldn't breathe
I felt deceived.
He gasped for air
But none was there.
He was rushed to the hospital
It was an emergency call.
He had a collapsed lung
I felt very hurt—truly stung.
He was on Lasix and Morphine
But his senses remained keen.
He tried to walk the hall
But instead he took a fall.
And with a sigh
I wonder "WHY?"

I thought this was it
But there was more.
The staff was really trying
To get to the core.
He was up in Englewood
Up on the fifth floor.
With internal problems
We could no longer ignore.
After his stumble
He had gotten very sore.
His health was very poor
And with a sigh
I asked "WHY?"

They took more X-Rays
Within the next few days.
So sore were his bones
All he did was moan and groan.
Another problem was his heart
It was not working and blood wouldn't part.

Fluid remained on his feet
At times looking red as a beet.
His arteries weren't pumping well
Thus causing everything to swell.
Most days he wouldn't eat
Thus causing us a lot of heat.
And with an irate sigh
I scream "WHY?"

He died on the final day of the year
With everybody shedding a tear.
The priest came again early that morn
Blessing him, before the family starts to mourn.
He lived to see Grandma's 88th birthday
Dying under the sun's ray.
He died during this Most Holy Season
Although I could not find the reason.

At present I knew he is in God's hands
Now listening to some of his favorite bands.
I hope he died without suffering, I pray
Thus alleviating me of my dismay.
And with a calmer sigh
I still ponder "Why, Why, Why?"

Age 39
Jan. 1996

DON'T TAKE NO

I heard a funny song
It hit me like a prong
It was full of town rap
Saying I don't take no crap.

I'm just like a terd
Being a 40'ish nerd
Also I won't quit, quit
Cause I don't take no shit.

So again, I say—no crap
Even if I have to snap
If you are full of bull
Then take it and give a pull.

And I don't take no shit
Cause I'll surely have a fit
Lastly, I say I don't take no crap
Nowhere on the face of this map.

Age 40
Aug. 1996

MISERY—A RAY OF HOPE

Misery arrives in many forms
As in the recent Quebec & Southern storms;
It visits no matter if you're black or white
Because at one time everyone seems to fight.

Misery can start with that first drink
Spending foolishly instead of buying mink;
For some it come in learning Math
While others are dying in a blood bath.

Misery can make a person cry
While most of them ask a simple "WHY"
In winter it'll bring on snow
Too often, a much uninvited foe.

Misery even creeps while people inhale & smoke
Accompanied by a resounding choke;
It haunts the neighbors as people steal
It makes the poor often miss a meal.

Misery will make some imbibe
Yet others go out and try to bribe;
It travels with many a twisted path
Bringing with it a lot of wrath.

Misery joins the hot sun and cooling rain
Yet driving some to go insane;
It disguises itself with depression & lows
Seeing the unemployed with no dough.

Misery can even come from animal bites
And also with some humans having no rights;
It'll cause honest people to go broke
While others get ill, and no longer joke.

Misery often teases with a deadly crush
Sometimes even through a cocaine rush;
It comes with all sorts of pain
Bringing to many a lot of disdain.

Misery betrays a marriage with adultery
Thus plunging couples into deep poverty;
All over people are lost on the Big Map
While children cry on their mother's lap.

Misery haunts with the sight of blood
And varied foreign countries facing a flood;
It hurts us will the touch of a fork prong
While others cannot even sing a melodious song.

Misery invades with many a lie
Letting the elderly wander, go off and die;
It still stifles teens learning geometry
While many die eating rotten poultry.

Misery at present shows off in the dorms
While sad folks at the funerals mourn;
Sometimes it's demonstrated in the bull rink
As moms slave over the kitchen sink.

Misery expels itself in the state of fire
Instead of manifesting from God's lyre;
It emits those with vericose veins
And even the handicapped using canes.

Misery attacks the people that are old
It then shows when they are cold;
It approaches before a doctor's shot
Making ones blood boil and remain hot.

Misery continues to endure
Certainly knowing how to gnaw;
It matures during icy cold and scalding heat
As well as on tired, achy feet.

Misery contains blow after blow
And the answer no—one seems to know;
It deprives some of dear sight
And others of beautiful daylight.

Misery replaces a bed with a cot
While the impoverished don't have a pot;
Misery seems to have many a flaw
At times, there seems to be no cure.

Misery seems to have us all beat
It appears to be an unconquerable feat;
It's made its' own ugly mold
In fact, Misery can be quite bold.

Misery appears on many a stage
Causing some to start a rage;
It manifests a lot in breaking the law
Like robbing goods from a store.

Misery is making us more bleak
Leaving us all up the creek;
It comes when one breaks a bone
It shows off in many an animalistic moan.

Misery never knows how to fade
In fact, it continues to invade;
It robs us of a kiss and a hug
It continues to grab and tug.

Misery will undo a marriage knot
And hemophiliacs blood can't clot;
It approaches with old age
While others don't earn a decent wage.

Misery is a loss instead of a win
As you can tell, it has many a sin;
It'll send the dizzy to the floor
Just like crime, it seems to soar.

Misery has gotten a firm hold
Having street gangs rob precious gold;
It causes sunburn skin to peel
It carries with it a mighty seal.

Misery leaves many people alone
It emits a horrific, terrible tone;
It teaches the poor how to mug
Also, agonizes with the bite of a bug.

Misery encroaches the elderly turning frail
While others sit and wait for their turn in jail;
It hits with the weight of a brick
Making many different people sick.

Misery is as cold as a piece of ice
It gives some a head full of lice;
It has no qualities like humble or meek
Yet it's as big and huge as Pike's Peak.

Misery in its form so pure
Is like a tremendous lion's roar;
While others continue to go and kill
It makes life seem all up hill.

Misery can start from a shot of gin
While families fight with their kin;
Nowadays it's in the newest flick
And causes pain from a pin prick.

Misery will make students fret and fail
As the drunkards sip and drink their ale;
Many ways it is set in stone
It makes some injuries prone.

Misery comes in the form of a raid
It causes some to be underpaid;
It'll make some want to flee
While the infirm drink their tea.

Misery has many a vice
Making all of us pay a price;
For some old apartment roofs leak
While the dirty smell and reek.

Misery puts us up to test
At times we cannot even rest;
It creeps up with noise and din
Giving some ears of tin.

Misery makes many loose their will
It brings morn and eve traffic to a standstill;
It leaves the faint, skinny and pale
While subways demonstrate a bloody trail.

Misery makes some swallow pills
While others get all sorts of ills;
It will skin a child's wounded knee
And yet it never seems to set us free.

Misery can be a staple of only rice
To some it brings a house full of mice;
It separates the worst from the best
Yet brings forth many a pest.

Misery causes shipwrecks at sea
It upturns and uproots a tree;
It causes children to tell long tales
While the elderly have moans and wails.

Misery never seems to know any hush
It continues to crush and crush;
All this above makes me want to reel
While Mother Teresa, the Cardinal and Pope kneel.

It's high time we start to feel
And use the Bible to help us heal;
It is no longer the hour to jibe
Thus instead listening to our Higher Scribe.

It's finally time that we start to fly
Instead of bending over and giving a sigh;
It's the season to mature and grow
Letting only God's Word flow.

We have to start to become real
Just like a raised, embossed seal;
Each of us must set our sight
Using the Holy Trinity as Our Light.

Age 40
Sept. 1996

CYCLOPES

One eyed—disease
removed, replaced by rubbery
one in place—Moves real—
But slithers like an eel
And still detachable.
At times, rotates like the
earth on its axis,
goes upside down
with gray matter showing.
Foreign matter enters daily
Like goo or pus
holds tight near the nose.

Age 40
Sept. 1996

Rage

*Rage is
Irate anger
Seething &
Pouring
Out like the
Venom of a
Snake*

RAGE

*Age 40
Nov 1996*

JEANNE'S ROOMMATE

I have a genius in the house
Who, at times, can be a louse
And is no longer like a mouse.

She talks a blue streak
She's no longer meek
For attention she seems to seek.

She asks and asks and asks
She gives everyone her tasks
And somehow has many masks.

She drives us all nuts
Still sometimes get in ruts
Yet she has as a lot of guts.

She knows how to manipulate
At times manifests a lot of hate
But she is never, ever, late.

She is truly a pest
Giving no one a rest
And putting everyone to the test.

She enjoys being crazy
Her life seems to be hazy
And she is quite lazy.

This year she's is extremely blue
Her friends limited to a few
But her ideas are always new.

Age 40
Jan 1997

CATS

Cats are such unique creatures
With long tails & whiskers as special features.
They come in various shapes and sizes
With a lot winning medals and prizes.
They come and go and eat and sleep as they please
They flit and flutter like a feather in the breeze.
They show that they are independent
They rub and rub to leave their scent.
Cats find every nook and cranny for their nap(s)
But most enjoy their companion's lap(s).
Some are finicky, others eat everything
Some are quiet, to others surprises they may bring.
They hunt and stalk and kill their prey
Most of all, cats love to play.
Cats will use string, paper, mice and balls
You can buy a purebred from the malls.
Although some have to go to vets
Cats make such great and wonderful pets.

Age 40
Jan 1997

HONORING
HIS HOLINESS
POPE JOHN PAUL II

Your ordination is now one plus fifty
For His Holiness, who is oh, so nifty.
The Holy Father, we wish you a Happy Anniversary
One that is prayerful, joyous and carefree.
You have reached a mighty milestone
To all, you are so very well known.
You are really the people's Pope
Always offering us some hope.
You are back in your native Poland
Bring out the orchestra, strike up the band.
You plan to travel to many a city
And yes, at times, you are quite witty.
You've come for the 'Statio Urbis'
And of plans which you'll furbish.
You are a unique man, indeed so humble
Please help us not to fail and stumble.
People have come from near and far
Just like the Magi following the Star.
You come with such a brilliant mind,
Holy Father and Pontiff, you are one of a kind.

Age 40
Jan 1997

AFTERTHOUGHTS OF A RETREAT

I went to bed last night
Thinking of many a Godly sight.
I heard the rain gently pitter-patter
It had to be God's soft-spoken chatter.
He had blest us with a warm summer day
Letting all soak up the sun's rays.
God also disguises Himself in heavy fog
And when in disgust, demonstrates smut & smog.
God reveals His wondrous grandeur and beauty
In every carved mountain and varied tree.
It's shown with a pet dormant on your bed
Sometimes with a child's laughter or a tear shed.
He presents Himself in people who sing
Actually Our Lord God is in Everything.
At times he tells us to Be Still
And just listen to His Holy Will.

Age 40
Feb 1997

A LENTEN REFLECTION

I wanted to write a Lenten Reflection
It's just a simple and quick meditation.
Lent begins on each Ash Wednesday
With old habits to be thrown away.
Lent can be a trying and tumultuous time
Like a child giving up his precious dime.
It's a time of severe repentance
And a true examination of conscience.
We are to pray, abstain and fast
Also to meditate on God's Past.

Age 40
Feb 1997

THE STORY OF GAMBLING FRANK

Frank likes to go to the track
Where he spends all his money;
This is his biggest flaw and crack
Instead of finding a nice honey.

Even better, he likes the Casinos
He's forever in Atlantic City;
Though the machines are his worst foes
And during poker ups the ante.

I heard he likes 5 card porker
With 2 pair or 3 of a kind;
In this there is no joker
Yet winning is hard to find.

One's ultimate goal is the Royal Flush
However, it is quite rare;
It surely gives one a quick rush
By upping the ante.

Frank always loses big and still bets
He seems to bring a lot of dough;
Which causes him grief and debts
Frank just can't seem to say "No".

Machines, cards, roulette & dice
They are found all over;
By losing, Frank will be eating rice
Poor Frank, where's his four leaf clover??

Age 41
March 1997

WINTERS LAST STAND

It was early March
I saw a black crow
He searched for food
But only found snow.

With little snow amounts
The plows didn't even blow
The roads were finally ice
Poor thing, had no place to go.

As usual I pitied him
For he was hungry too
The roads were cold and bare
With crumbs too far and few.

He looked, searched and pecked
But only came up dry
For him, nothing was found
As winter decided to say "GOODBYE".

Age 41
March 1997

DEFINITION OF A SAINT

A Saint is a person
Who is a true friend.
A person there through good & bad
And sees all things till the end.

A Saint is someone
Who is always very true.
They never turn their back
Even if you're down and blue.

A Saint is your companion
Always cleaning up your mess.
They are there for every tear
A person comforting your distress.

A Saint does everything you say
Listens to all your commands.
They have cauliflower ears
Absorbing the strangest demands.

A Saint is a genuine gem
Holding all mixed emotions.
They help, lead, assist & guide
If stopped, they put you in motion.

A Saint is brought about by God
Wearing an invisible halo.
They come to cheer & bring "Good News"
No matter where we plan to go.

A Saint never strays too far
They are always at your side.
If faltering or in trouble
Your saint'll never ever hide.

Age 41
April 1997

BLOCKED SUNBLOCK

I wanted to use my Coppertone bottle
From a winter's drought, it was constipated.
I shook, pushed & squeezed
Nothing emitted—perhaps being outdated.

It really seemed so darn strange that—
The aloe just wouldn't budge.
Finally I gave it a toothpick enema
Which unclogged the aloe hard as fudge.

We pushed it again harder
Thus it emitted like diarrhea.
It went all over Jean & the car
So badly that she couldn't steer.

She laughed so hard that
She emitted tears dripping.
About a blue constipated bottle
Which in a drawer lie sitting.

Age 41
June 1997

POLAND

Poland—a land of flat plain
   Flat like the Meseta of Spain.
Poland—a country where poppies abound
   Also where religious garb is still found.
Poland—the birthplace of the Pope
   Who offers every nation rays of hope.
Poland—the homeland of the Salt Mines
   And also that of LOT Airlines.
Poland—home of Potatoes and Pierogi
   Home of the monetary zloty.
Poland—a country of Beets and Kielbasi
   Also famous for snowy Zakopane.
Poland—a land plentiful in Amber and Silver
   And homeland to the Vistula River.
Poland—a country whose capital is Warsaw
   A country where al the town hall artists draw.
Poland—with a city named Krakow
   Where the proverb is "Later—Not Now".
Poland—home to a town called Giezno
   Unfortunately, home also to economic woe.
Poland—where Auschwitz still cries
   Upon looking one can hear people sighs.
Poland—birthplace of St. Stanislaus
   And of the revered icon of Jasna Gora.
Poland—home of the Eucharistic Congress in Wroclaw
   Home to where many a beautiful peacock caw
Poland—a land part called Silesia
   Home to yet a very visible militia.
Poland—the birthplace of Copernicus and Chopin
   The land were the capital was once Poznan.
Poland—the land of the renowned Solidarity
   And of humble people who share generosity.

Age 41
June 1997

JOHN DENVER

It was 5:30 on Columbus Day
Supposedly in an All-American way
Parties, feasts, parades
Yet, it turned out to be un-American
Very sad, chilling and ironic
John Denver passed on near Monterrey
He died "Leaving on a Jet Plane".
For he wrote tunes so patriotic
He died to many's disdain
He left with "Sunshine on his Shoulders".
He died amidst those mighty Rocky Boulders
Thank God he was a "Country Boy".
His music never looked to annoy
But did bring a lot of joy
So dearest God up above
"Take John Home via Country Road,
Passing West Virginia," then to his abode.

Age 41
Oct. 1997

THE HEAT WAVE

Summer is finally here at last
It comes on with a fury and fast.
Just like a firecracker's blast
It seems to be worse than the past.

Clothes are off, they're in a heap
It's so darn hot, I cannot sleep.
Into the pool, all kids leap
While the farmers sweat and reap.

I feel sorry for my cat
His fur is like a mat.
Everyone seems to don a sun hat
For some, we are shedding our fat.

For the elderly, this is a nightmare
To venture out, they don't dare.
The hazy sun is giving off glare
So we all cut & shorten our hair.

Ozone levels are way too high
While the east states cook and fry.
Most people yawn and sigh
Some may even fall and die.

Forecasters predict more on the way
It's El Nino, El Nino they repeatedly say.
The grass now looks like burnt hay
Please, not too much longer, people pray.

Temps are raging up to a hundred
When out, bald men are turning red.
It's so bad, I can't sleep in bed
I wish it were a bit cooler instead.

Age 42
June 1998

THE FACE OF MISERY

Day in and day out
I see the poor people pout,
I read stories of deadly gout.
There's a lot of futuristic doubt.
This is the face of misery.

On earth it's a living hell
Everyone has a tale to tell.
The homeless carry a foul smell
Too many jailed in one cell
And the elderly seem less well.
Thus; the face of agony.

I see the anger of the ill
Everyone has had their fill.
The dead lie stoically still
While others prepare a will
Then some decide to take a pill.
This is the face of misery.

A lot of elderly no longer hear
And others can no longer steer.
There abounds a lot of fear
Hubbies no longer call their mates "Dear"
And even God is not too clear.
Thus; the face of agony.

One person has a tumor in his brain
Some slip in the pouring rain
So many seem to be in pain
Especially those dying in a plane.
While politicians lie in vain.
This is the face of misery.

The unfulfilled vent their steam
And they force a fake gleam.
You see the tears of a broken dream
Like not being part of a team
Or a child not having ice cream.
Thus; the face of agony.

Students continually flunk.
The Vietnam Vet lies in a funk.
Babies are found in the back trunk.
While streets are lined with junk
And all morals seem to have sunk.
This is the face of misery.

Danger comes from the bumblebee
Children are now latchkey
There is no more solidarity
So our men go on lines of infantry
And politics is full of baloney.
Thus; the face of agony.

Farmers have little or no grain
While a new dress gets a stain.
Drought turns to heavy rain
Harsh words are spoken in vain
And anarchy begins to reign.
This is the face of misery.

This is the era of The Mob
When mothers begin to sob
Then a father loses his job,
And the thief continues to rob
While the disheveled are considered a slob.
Thus; the face of misery.

With nowadays jobs—gone are the frills
But mounting yet are steady bills
Immigrants stare out window sills
We have to climb many hills
To face life's nasty drills.
Such is the face of agony and misery!

AGONY

I go to bed crying
each and every night
Knowing mom drinks
And dad still fights.

I'm upset with a lot
Grandma growing old,
My lack of patience
Perhaps living in the cold.

God taught us peace
But there's always a war
Bombs being dropped
My mind is battered and sore.

I look forward to my pets
They live in perfect harmony.
They nurture each of their young
And they live a life so carefree.

It might be wrong for a Catholic
Not to believe in Hell
Yet after the earthly pain
Our afterlife has to be swell.

Age 42
Sept. 1998

BROKEN HEART

I have a broken lonely heart
Mine is oh, so torn apart.
I am hurt and wretched
Feeling like a lowly vetch.
Mom now drinks 'round the clock
Seems as if God deserted His flock.
Not too many seem to care
And therefore, my temper flares.
Recently life has turned into a mess
With all abandoning and no one to caress.
Mom now drinks 'round the clock
Seems as if God deserted His flock.
My lifelong battle is downhill
I've just about had my fill.
Everyone and Everything is such a disaster
That I wonder if God is truly my Master.

Age 42
Oct. 1998

AH, THE RAISE

I got a raise, got a raise!
See hard work really pays.
Now I can buy that vase
And see a lot of plays.

Yes I got a raise, got a raise
Can't just sit there in a gaze.
Wasting away precious days
For I really deserve the praise.

I got a raise, got a raise
It is like a sugary coat of glaze.
Now I'll work like a fiery blaze
And never sit there in a daze.

Now I gotta change my ways
Not for now, but always.
Better act like happy blue jays
Just cause I got a raise.

Age 42
Nov. 1998

Y

Y is such a crooked letter
Y can't the world be better?
Y do we have so much crime
Especially in this day and time?
Y is the earth round
And yet chop meat ground?
Y do some people joke and tease
Only to make our nerves freeze?
Y do we decide to dress
When we're in such distress?
Y does my belly ache
Every time I act like a flake?
Y do cats and dogs die
While birds soar high?
Y is such a crooked letter
So why does winter get wetter?
Y do we suffer with a cold
And then finally grow old?
Y do we complain
About the wise and insane?
Y do some get so crazy
When others are so lazy?
Y do people get a stroke
While others are poor and broke?
Y is such a crooked letter
That I wish I were an Irish Setter!

Age 42
Nov. 1998

WHY

I ask WHY—
Why is there sickness
As opposed to health?
Why is there poverty
As opposed to wealth?
Why are there no answers
To those who have various cancers?
I query Why?
Why are our hearts cold
As opposed to warm?
And why do we injure
And look to cause harm?
I scream Why?
Why aren't our thoughts
clean instead of impure?
Why do we have such
hardships to endure?
I fret Why?
Why do we have
a blue moon—
Instead of seeing
the glistening stars?
And why does God
Seem to be so far?
My lips tremble Why—
Why aren't there people
in the vast crowd
Even when I hear
Screams out loud?

Age 42
Nov 1998

THAT'S MARY RAUSCH

She leads with a gentle hand
Does everything as planned;
Yet takes a firm stand
That's Mary Rausch!

To the parish, she's precious
For her faith, ferocious.
To everyone near, gracious
And she's very vivacious;
That's Mary Rausch!

She's no potato on a couch
And never ever a grouch;
To this we can all vouch
That's Mary Rausch!

She says her Rosary
With her partner, Larry.
Her views do not vary
And she never seems to wary.
That's Mary Rausch!

She's sweet and nice
Just like an Italian Ice.
She'll always share her slice.
That's Mary Rausch!

You'll find Mary in her pew
Praising the morning dew.
Now she's head of Renew.
That's Mary Rausch!

She does this for the Lord
Never seeking any reward
Thus was bestowed the Papal Award.
That's our Mary Rausch!

Age 42
Dec. 1998

OUR SAVIORS BIRTH

In a faraway place

Lay a manger

And unto the world

Cometh no stranger;

Today is the Day

Jesus, Our Lord is born

And now is the time

For us to adorn.

Age 42
Dec. 1998

MOUTH WATERING FOOD

First up that luscious soup
Just stare at the macaroni loop.
Munching on the Chef Salad
'Tis harmonious, like a ballad.
Then served up the garlicy pasta
Just remember enough is Basta!
Don't overcook the spaghetti
It'll look like confetti.

While cooking a succulent steak
Make sure to broil, never bake.
Tryin' a thigh of Boston Chicken
Remember it's food for good licken.
Taste buds aroused for sauteed veal
Seems to meet with mass appeal.
The kids are yearning for a hot dog
Roast it good over a fiery log.
Seem to be in a bit of a jam
Go out for a baked honey ham.

In the mood for a juicy fish
Don't forget the finger bowl dish.
It's Friday, time for a clam
Just check out where it swam!
Rather have a plate of tuna
It can't be here much sooner
Ready for a broiled crab
Ask for hot butter to dab.
And don't forget the stuffed shrimp
Not many, for your veins will crimp.

So you're gonna eat a fried egg
Better with coffee than a keg.
Yearning for a slice of cheese
It's something to munch on in a breeze.
Like to serve florets of broccoli?
Try 'em with a dip of guacamole.
When eating an ear of buttered corn
Remember its alias is horn.

Really stumped over a mushroom
Nah, it's only a fungus in bloom.
Pensive as to what goes with beets?
Just about any kind of meats.
How to get the kids to eat peas?
You better be on bended knees.
Is your favorite the carrot?
Munch and chew, but not near a parrot.

Dessert time with lemon meringue pie
It's absolute heaven in the sky.
Calories gathered in frosty cake
Just one mo' piece, for Pete's sake.
Perhaps you prefer Italian Ice
To the lips, oh so sweet and nice.
And for the finale, some ice-cream
Oh what a heavenly DREAM!!!

Age 43
Jan. 1999

MENOPAUSE

That Change of Life
Bringing you strife.
With hot flashes
And dizzying crashes.
Food binging
And nerves twinging.
Looking like a creep
Lying in a heap.
Moods swing
You feel like a king.
This crazy spell
Sending you to hell.
Mostly you weep
You can't sleep.
You get forgetful
And maybe regretful.
You're growing old
And starting to fold.

Age 43
March, 1999

You Don't Know

*You don't know
How much I miss
a motherly kiss;
A tender hand
that cares—
running through
my fine hair.
You don't know
how I hurt
to feel like dirt;
being a bad curse
instead of gold
tucked into a purse.
You just don't know!*

*You have no idea
of how my brain
is like sour beer
instilling fear—
horrible thoughts
yet trying hard
all for naught.
You just don't know
how miserable
I really am;
feeling like a
rancid clam
instead of a
pearly oyster.
Being compared to
an ugly monster.
No, you don't know
No-one knows.*

*Age 43
April 1999*

FUNERALS AND DEATH

They are so morbid and morose
But then
think again.
Look at the word—
There is a rose
Any colored rose
tons of 'em.
Signifying life
That beyond death
there is more;
A deeper, profound
beauty beyond.

Watching Littleton
taught me something.
Awe—inspiring
through provoking
moving and touching
words—Words
that'll heal.
In Colorado they
strive to feel
the pain of each other.
Sobs, prayers, actions
working together
to pick up the torches
of those who fell.
Fell to death—
No—No
Rose to eternal
Life—Life BEYOND.

Age 43
April 1999

RECEPTIONIST

With phone
on my breast
And naked body
I call you.
With silky bubbles
on my slithery body
I try to catch up
On daily phone calls.
I converse while
caressing one leg
then the other;
continuing upward
toward tummy, arm
and finally face.
I reach for towel,
dry off, all within
the realm of politics,
news notes, strikes.
Such is 90's life.
A rat race, stress
Eating on the run
and the like.

Age 43
Aug. 1999

ME/WORLD

I'm in such a mess
With lots of undo stress
And under severe duress.

I can't seem to cope
And lose all rays of hope
Ya'all saying (I'm a dope.)

Knowing I'm a freak
My future seems bleak
And thus I'm getting weak.

I've had my fill
Of trudging up hill
Fighting life's drills.

At times I just give up and sigh
And tell the world, "Good Bye"
Before I finally die.

I want to return Home
Where I'm free to roam
Under His Blue Dome.

Oh God, please take me
Liberate and set me free
For I am bitter and angry.

Age 43
Aug 1999

HAPPIER TIMES

I cannot remember nor recall
Any of my recent happy times
I don't need ringing or a daily phone call
Regarding my Mom's alcoholic crimes.
I'm tired of seeing my dad
Going thru her purse
Knowing he too is sad
From this alcoholic, devilish curse.

Oh God, where are those happier days
Days at sunny Bridge, weeks in Puerto Rico
Times when we were all happy and gay
Even when we were roasted in Mexico?
I wish I were back in Saints
Getting A's in Latin and Spanish.
Those happier times that weren't tainted
Even if I did poorly in English!

My life has never been the same
With gin, vodka and scotch taking the reign
And I'm told that I'm to blame
No wonder I have such stomach pains.
What ever happened to Prohibition?
Why are our laws so Darn LAX?
Why don't more people take action?
These are the questions, where are the facts?

Age 42
Aug 1999

ALONE

I am the only fish in the sea
For everyone has abandoned me.

I am distressed, sad and blue
With absolutely nothing to do.

The minutes in bed tick away
The hours pass day by day.

For I'm slowly drowning
That's why I'm always frowning.

Please come back to my side
And help me to restore my pride.

Age 43
Sept 1999

FLOYD

Floyd's turned our lives upside down
Some being evacuated from town
So everyone's wearing a frown.

He's unleashed his wrath
From Jersey to the Carolina path
Making all redo their math.

He's emptied our schools
And turned yards into pools.

The gardeners are finally mowing
But our rivers are overflowing
So residents use canoes for rowing.

He's played havoc with our power
And has turned our water sour.

We all seem to moan
Since we can't use the phone
Because there is no tone.

So everyone's quite annoyed
And no-one is overjoyed
With Hurricane Floyd.

Age 43
Sept. 1999

THE WEIRD WORLD

The world is weird
Weird being one feature;
Attacking both male and female
Just about every creature.

The world is weird
People kill every day;
I wish I could grow wings
And just fly far, far away.

The world is weird
With all sorts of addictions;
Drugs, alcohol and sex
So we need better restrictions.

The world is weird
And most are so crazy;
With Satan at the reigns
I wish I were a daisy.

The world is weird
With bombs being hurled;
And hate exceeding love
It'll make your hair uncurl.

Age 43
Nov. 1999

DOREEN KOVACH

SOLEMN FAREWELL

We'll hate to see you go
But I guess it's God's will;
We loved your Masses and homilies
You surely were a thrill.

With your wit, we'd be amused
And you had the broad Irish smile;
You joked, cajoled and were jolly
It was just your style.

On Sundays you lectured the people
Sitting in the array of pews;
You were stern and firm
But never blew your fuse.

You had it in for Koch
He had it in for you;
You both went to court
But you wouldn't sue!

We didn't need a Sr. Act
For you were a one man show;
We surely are gonna' hate
To see you go.

You stood for every parade
Shaking many a strangers' hand;
You had a unique and special way
Which was truly, truly grand.

You loved the Yankees
We know you were quite a fan;
Just remember we all love you
'Cause you have been and are a special
Man.

We love you dearly
Like a kid's teddy bear;
So go in God's peace
And please take care.

Age 43
Dec. 15, 1999

UNDESERVED LOVE

You are our boss
who died upon the cross.
You died to save us from sin
and to renew us again.
You plant little seeds
so we may do Great Deeds.
Even if we don't straighten our Path
God; you don't bestow your Total Wrath.
It is you for which we long
even when we are wrong.

Age 44
March 2000

A SPECIAL LADY

Mary Raush is very special
She has a lot of talent
Mary Raush is kind of unique
Helpful, wise and gallant.

To St. John's, she belongs
And her willpower is strong
If you have to grieve
You can do it on Mary's sleeve.

I must confess
She listens with an open ear
Her patience is endless
That's a sign of Mary dear.

With Mary you'll never be ignored
Because she lives so deeply with the Lord
And therefore, the KOC board
Is bestowing her another award.

Age 44
March, 2000

THE SEVEN GIFTS

I'm yearning for Wisdom
so I may enter His Kingdom.
I'm searching for Understanding
That I may be less Demanding.
I asked God for Council
So I could be His Stencil.
I asked for a lot of Fortitude
So that He can change my Attitude.
I'm craving more Knowledge
And much deeper than that of college.
I'm begging for Piety
That I my live with Society.
I already have Fear of the Lord
For He's the chief—Head of the Board.
These are the seven gifts of the Holy Spirit
So come one and all, SHARE IT AND SPREAD IT.

Age 44
June 2000

HAIL MARY

Hail Mary, Full of Grace
Mother and Queen of the human race.

The Lord is with Thee
Queen of earth and of the sea.

Blest are those amongst women
For you carried our future omen.

And blest is the fruit
Hallowed with flute.

Of your womb, Jesus
Protector of the unborn fetus.

Holy Mary, Mother of God
You gave Him a perfect nod.

Pray for us sinners now
As you did take a solemn vow.

And at the hour of our death
As we take our final breath.

Amen.

Age 44
May 2000

WEST/EAST

I went out west
And found a slower pace.
Nothing like the east
A total rat race.

The people are calmer
There is less stress;
But I like home better
I really must confess.

Their days are a scorcher
Their sun is like Spain.
When my legs got burnt
It really was a pain.

Things are more expensive
Though I don't know why;
Yet I got things on sale
So I really can't cry.

Age 44
May 2000

DOREEN KOVACH

CALIFORNIA

I wanted to leave
To get away;
I went to Redwood City
Near San Francisco Bay.

It was partly
A disaster;
Her being far worse
Than my master.

"Put jewelry away,
and make your bed".
I heard the orders
Those of which I dread!

I went to San Fran
And saw the cable cars;
I wanted a side trip
To see Hollywood stars.

I saw many
A beautiful site;
And her cat April
At times, did bite.

Aunt Betty made me
Wild rice and pork.
She told me to break
An egg without a fork!

She absolutely hated
That four letter word;
And I couldn't stand
Casey, the weird bird.

I went to spend and rest
For a perfect vacation;
It almost seems like
I was offering an oblation.

Age 44
May 2000

In Despair

There are times it
seems I can't cope;
I'm losing it all
all signs of hope.

I search and search
in and out all day;
My life is in such
a messy disarray.

No Jeannie, Eric or Jerry
No more friends;
Just seems like my
Rope is at its end.

All of the above
came and went;
So I use my
mouth to vent.

I pray and pray
all night and day;
that the Lord God
can show me the way.

Age 44
June 2000

DOREEN KOVACH

THE SICK WORLD

The man who dropped the brick
He was ill, very, very sick.

Yet there are others;
Some can be mothers,
Fathers, sisters, or brothers.

They're in the midst of society
With some lacking sobriety
And others not having piety.

Life today is a sick game
Religion is not the same
With everyone using the Lord's name.

Some rob, cheat, and steal
At work, they wheel and deal
And others refuse to kneel.

Kids are out to kill
After they had there fill
Because life is all up hill.

Life today is such a stress
I confess, No—one could care less
Indeed, we're in a mess.

This sick world is a maze
With the ME—EGO in a daze
And drugged kids' eyes in a gaze.

Age 44
July 2000

PERSONA

I am a mask
I seek attention.
I glow and bask
By causing dissension.

I am such a beast
which howls and screams.
I have a tasty feast
By killing your dreams.

Like the brain of Castro
I am a mask.
Like a messy "Rastro"
Everything is a task.

I am a witch
Both wicked and evil
at times also a snitch
A character so febrile.

I am a hideous leach
I gnaw and gnaw.
True friends I breach
By flaw after flaw.

Yes, I am this mask
Like the poisonous venom
seeping thru a flask
I am a demon.

Age 44
July 2000

P.M., P.S.

I am nocturnal
Just like an owl;
Only difference, I'm quiet
And do not howl.

Many a night I pray
Or try to count sheep;
Along comes an idea
So with a pen, I leap!

The subject doesn't matter
Each is a personal diary.
Depending on my mood
Some may be fiery;

I ponder, think and write
While in my bed;
Then goes on the light
While I ought to sleep instead.

Age 44
July 2000

MONEY

With **Thai** *Baht*—*you can get a floor cot.*
Some **Venezuelan** *Bolivar*—*to dine on caviar.*
With **Jordan's** *Dinar*—*nothing could be finer!*
The worthy **American** *Dollar*—*Sh—don't holler!*
Some **Greek** *Drachma*—*go talk to Grandma.*
German's *Deutchmark*—*to spend in Berlin's Park.*
With **Portuguese** *Escudo*—*change your pseudo.*
Enough of **Hungary's** *Forent*—*will get you to Greece's Corinth.*
French & Swiss *Franc*—*enough and you're swank!*
Netherlands *Guilder*—*to be a builder.*
Denmark and Norway's *Krone*—*fine for the phone.*
Czeck *Koruna*—*got enough for tuna?*
Turkish and Italian *Lire*—*oh baby-come nearer.*
U.S. *Dimes and Nickels*—*can buy me a few pickles.*
The **Spanish** *Peseta*—*useful on Madrid's Meseta.*
Some **So. American** *Pesos*—*will lead to a few besos.*
England's *Pound*—*is still quite sound.*
Ireland's *Punt*—*can send you on a bear hunt.*
So. Africa's *wealthy* **Rand**—*to buy a unique wedding band.*
Enough **Indian** *Rupee*—*you'll have some whoopee.*
Austria's *Schilling*—*a lot for a theater billing.*
Israeli *Shekel*—*can rid you of Dr. Jeckel.*
One or two **Korean** *Won*—*will buy a bon-bon.*
With **Chinese** *Yuan*—*you can be Juan.*
The **Japanese** *Yen*—*is fun to buy a hen.*
Some **Polish** *Zloty*—*is useful for the public potty.*

Age 44
July 2000

THE PAPAL PASS

Please wear your Pass
All thru the city of Rome
If not—it's a trespass
Under St. Peter's Dome!

Oh, we needed a pass
A pass here and there
One for food, Even Mass
Just about one for everywhere!

Oh, the darn pass
We had to show it all about
It showed that we class
And to a certain extent—clout!

Oh, any colored pass
On foot or on bus
To enter Tor Vergata grass
Even if it was a fuss.

Oh, the heavenly pass
For the Vatican
To see a musical or concerto brass
Whether you were black, white, or tan.

The pass, the pass, the pass
For metro or train
It was a gas
And drove us insane!

Age 44
Aug. 2000

HAKCENSACK LUNCH ON THE BENCH

I ate on a Hackensack bench
With all their awful stench.
I decided to munch
On my bolonga lunch.
I ate out 'cause of nice weather
While watching birds plume their feathers.
To the pigeons I fed
The ends of my bread.
At first only one or two
But then dozens flew.
I was waiting for the bus
Which at times isn't a plus.

Age 44
Aug. 2000

FEAR

Every night I walk the floor
Because I am so unsure
I never know what'll happen
I try to sleep and then
Harried thoughts invade my mind
Like my brain is in a bind.
I think of this or that
And occasionally hear the spat
I hate to go to bed
After all that was said.
My heart and stomach pound
Knowing that Ma will still hound.

Age 44
Sept. 2000

THE SUMMIT

The theme of the summit is world peace
Obviously all participants want war to cease.
It is being held in New York at the United Nations
We hope there won't be any fierce altercations.
Tuesday, September 5th, began the millennial summit
It was enough to make some people vomit.
Wednesday saw the display of Castro
It turned out to be as messy as a Rastro.
Tomorrow promises a lot of demonstrations
So people should use mass transportation.
Tomorrow is today and there is even more congestion
Due to the Hip-Hop Music Award Convention.
East side, West side, there was gridlock
Cars bumper to bumper, each and every block.
Clinton and Castro decided to have a handshake
I just hope it was sincere and not fake.

Age 44
Sept. 2000

THE SUMMER THAT WASN'T

This was the summer
that was truly a bummer.
It was rather cool
and too damp for the pool.
There was way too much rain
which drove us insane.
Galoshes were our main gear
in this 2000th year.
At some point, we ran for cover
while others went to the movies with their lover.
It wasn't a bit of fun
hardly even seeing the sun.

Age 44
Sept. 2000

THANK YOU

Thank you, thank you
for acknowledging me.
Yes, I am human
and not a tree.
I may act silly
and a bit immature.
But I'm trying to change
this is for sure.

Age 44
Oct 2000

OUR MAXINE

Ah, Maxine
Our Feline;
Stay by my breast
And take a nice rest.
Take a quick catnap
On mom or dad's lap.
Roll over and play dead
In the midst of my bedspread.
Ah-Maxine,
Our Queen;
Stretched and long
To us, you belong.

Age 44
Dec 2000

DON'T GO

Don't ever go on the pond
Where there is ice.
You may fall in
Which won't be too nice.

You may want
To try to skate,
But you are really
Tempting your fate.

In you'll go and
sink pretty fast;
Leaving some bystanders
With faces aghast.

Age 44
Dec. 2000

The Blowing Winds

The wind continues to blow
Yet the sky is all aglow
And it feels like it may snow.

It's finally December
and a time to remember
The Yule log embers.

December 5th is the coldest
night of the year.
Even though the sky
is very clear.

I'm starting to shiver
As goose bumps make me quiver.
Any day we'll have some snow
Because the winds are starting to blow.

Age 44
Dec. 2000

MIXED EMOTIONS

The snow is gently falling
winter is in full swing;
People bustle here and there
in preparation of the Majestic King.

The Menorah is lit
Ramadan is in full gear;
Stores thrive and Santa abounds
But do we really celebrate with cheer?

Pilgrims had to rearrange
their travel and air plans;
There were too many atrocities
so Christmas left the Holy Land.

It's a horror to see sibling rivalry
And other people's oppression;
The days are shortest
Causing the worst depression.

I ran away to be happy
to stitch, pray and reflect;
I ran from a home that
is ravaged with conflict.

I got a phone message
"Happy Holidays", it said;
It should have stated
That I should "DROP DEAD".

Age 44
Dec 23, 2000

PROBLEMS

Economic woes
Stay away from foes.
Got job loss—
Stay far from the boss.
Loss of self-esteem—
Blow off some steam.
Poor eyesight?
Stay out of the sunlight.
Can't loose weight—
Don't eat a full plate.
Always on drugs?
You need a few hugs.
Got lots of bills
And wanna take PILLS??
Gonna be in a mess
If you have a lot of stress.

These are all troubles
That come from burst bubbles.

Age 44
Dec. 2000

YEAR'S END

'Tis the finale of the year
this the end of the millennium;
Let's all celebrate with cheer
And not any chaos or bedlam.

I'd like to send a clear plea
of no alcohol or drugs;
Let the parties be problem free
And without riotous thugs.

Let the ball drop
Let Dick hold the show;
Don't let your feet stop
And let the sequins glow.

The church bells will chime
Every adult and child will cheer;
Let's all wish for less crime
Along with less fear.

Age 44
Dec. 30, 2000

NEW YEAR'S 2001

The Pope asked for peace
that wars may cease.
In Tokyo the bells chimed
While I sat and rhymed.
Russia was like a future page
With glowing beams being the rage.
Ali dropped the ball
While Dick Clark made the call.
All the revelers counted down to one
Although cold, they had a lot of fun.

Age 44
Jan. 1, 2001

IT'S HARD TO COMPREHEND

It is hard to comprehend
the thoughts of an ex-friend.
No matter what, she didn't budge
and is like a piece of hard fudge.
We both went to Seton Schools,
so neither of us should be fools.
I want so hard to have her back
and no longer wish to give her slack.

Age 44
Jan. 1, 2001

I WONDER

Does God answer prayer
Does He really care?
I often wonder What, Why and How
We still have problems here and now.
I wonder about this and that
I question, "Who's got my Welcome Mat?"
Why don't enough caress
Yet everyone wants to possess?
Yes, what does God think
When His eyes look and blink?

Age 44
Jan. 2001

THE CAT

The Cat is a simple animal
Not asking for much;
Just a little water and food
And some human touch.

Felines in general are independent
If you stroke they clean their fur;
Stroke and pet them enough
They'll begin to purr.

Purring demonstrates happiness
They'll sleep on your lap;
They also love to roll and play
But especially like to nap.

They like mice and catnip
Also string and balls;
Our furry friends
Even play in the halls.

Age 44
Jan 2001

THE COLOUR SCHEME

The Chalice done in Gold
To make it look bold.
Wheat done in pale yellow
To signify Our Lord's wafer as mellow.
The Wafer done in ecru/white
That of which we take a bite.
The Corpus done in vibrant red
Showing that His Blood was shed.
Grapes done in wine
Symbolizing the blood sign.
The ladder done in brown
Alongside the Thorny Crown.
The Arch done in blue
Reminding us of Mary's hue.
Jewels being rubies, pearls, emeralds
All for a man whose been called.

Age 45
January 2001

GETTING ILL

Cold after cold
We get more
As we get old.

The Pneu and flu
Is striking more
Than a few.

They strike any race
Also young and old
And slows your pace.

Sometimes these diseases kill
It doesn't matter to whom
With the body lying still.

Age 44
Jan. 2001

ESPANA

Guapo Juan Carlos es el rey
Y tiene mucha fe
Cuando el Congreso pasa la Ley.

Su Senora es una dama
Que puede dormir en cama
Porque tiene mucha fama.

Madrid es el capital
Donde hay mucho sol
Y se juega futbol.

Tierra de muchos colores
Y de varias flores
Pero no muchos dolores.

Hay muchos catolicos
Ya pocos alcoholicos
Y ningunos comicos.

Age 44
Jan. 2001

CAT IN THE WINDOW

Cat in the window
pretty as can be;
Not a worry in the world
just content and carefree.

She sits idly by
while in her prime;
Watching squirrels and robins
passing her time.

When noticed she
jumps with ease;
Yet she always does
as she pleases.

She bounds down
with such agility;
Then rolls and purrs
with cat-ability!

Age 44
Jan 2001

THE GIANTS

The Giants won
But it wasn't fun.
They drew heavy blood first
That the Vikings needed a Hearst.

The score was 41-zip.
For the ball, they did grip.
They passed and scored
While the fans roared.

Next is onto the Super Bowl
Which has been their main goal.
Betters are calling their bookies
'cause the Giants are no rookies.

Everyone is flocking to OTB
Hoping to cash in on Giants glory.

Age 44
Jan 2001

OUR FATHER

Our Father, who art in heaven
Maker of all our brethren.

Hallowed be Thy Name
For no-one is quite the same.

Thy Kingdom come, and will be done
Whether under dome or sun.

On earth as it is in heaven
This earth which you made in seven.

Give us this day our daily bread
As the Holy Book hath said.

And forgive us our trespasses
As we approach the masses.

As we forgive those
Especially our foes.

Who trespass against us
Whether in car or bus.

And lead us not into temptation
But rather lead us to redemption.

But deliver us from evil
And also from the DEVIL.

Amen.

Age 44
Jan. 2001

AT LAST

Clinton is leaving at last
His tumultuous two terms have passed.

Many people he did employ
Yet a lot of troops he did deploy.

He left the economy stable
amidst many a fable.

True, strong he made the economy
But his rhetoric was baloney.

He had a lot of charm
Yet did a lot of harm.

At times he was stunning
and to the press cunning.

The president knew how to maneuver and weave
For many a trick, he had up his sleeve.

He had way too much sex
that now it is a hex.

Eight years of horrid trash
Bringing late night jokes in a flash.

These years brought about some turmoil
and with it, Monica's blue dress to soil.

There was a mess with Paula Jones
and more of it on the phones.

Jackson and Sharpton looked with awe
Even though Clinton had many a flaw.

He was caught and had to 'fess
In order to avoid a bigger mess.

So he left office in disgrace
As President Bush took his place.

Bush now takes the reigns
Amidst his predecessors stains.

At last we have some civility
With a man who has credibility.

Age 44
Jan 20, 2001

I'M SICK

Most of the time
I feel so sick;
My stomach is
Like a hard brick.

I can not speak
and remain mute;
For if I open my mouth
I'll get the boot.

I get nauseous
then want to vomit;
My stomach is like
A rotating comet.

I no longer can
eat a full meal;
'cause I never know
how I'll feel.

I worry 'bout this
I worry 'bout that;
I just don't have to
worry about getting fat!

Age 44
Feb 2001

AT DEATH'S DOORSTEP

Death—it causes the weak to stumble
and yet the faith-ful to be humble.
It can be life's worst pain
but in the end we all gain.
SIDS, murder, war lay
at the doorstep of death.
With old age and Alzheimer's
expiring one's last breath.
Death can come on a raging fire
making many inside quickly expire.

Age 44
Feb. 2001

TIME

Time is fleeting
While my heart is beating.
The seconds tick-tock
As I use my remote clock.
Thirty becomes twenty-nine
Which is still just fine.
Then it became twenty-eight
As time ticks away our fate.
Moving down to twenty-seven
Yet not approaching heaven.
Twenty-seven becomes twenty-six
Ugh—we're sure in a fix.
Twenty-six ticks to twenty-five
Time is really taking a dive.
Sixty strokes to twenty-four
As we each do a chore.
One less minute to twenty-three
And time has drifted to the sea.
Down, down to twenty-two
As I realize that my years are few.
Twenty-two becomes twenty-one
And thus time is becoming undone.
Yes, time marches on
With Hours, Minutes, and Seconds GONE.

Age 44
Feb 2001

SARAH HUGHES, THE BEST

O Dear Sarah, you're simply the best
That's why you were Great Neck's Honored Guest.

You have truly been blest
With a lot of vim, vigor & zest.

I really must confess
You've been put to the test.

You persisted & pressed
To reach your goal, your quest.

You've reached the pinnacle, the crest
By lots of practice, work & no rest.

And to be funny, I'll say in a jest
You never have the time to lay in the nest.

Age 44
2001

CHORES THAT BORE

Make the bed
then pull up spread.
Clean your dish
and feed the fish.
Answer the phone
while you mutter and moan.
Oh these chores
that are a darn bore.
Clean the table
then install a new cable.
Wash out the tub
and scrub and scrub.
Sort the mail
then file your nail.
Oh these chores
that are a darn bore.

Age 44
March 2001

HATE

I hate them
And they hate me.
And that's the way
It'll always be.

It is so hard
to really believe
that little ole me
she did conceive.

I have no freedom
He's like Franco,
Mussolini, Hitler,
and the whole Gestapo.

Dead is the best mood
I can describe.
I wish I had poison
so I could imbibe.

Age 44
March 10, 2001

OH DEAR GOD

Oh Dear God, please guide me
Show me Your Path;
For I am angered and full of hate
Please rid me of my wrath.

I'm so content here in Spain
Help me find The Way;
Straight or narrow, or twisted road
Reform, oh reform me to obey.

Lord, I'm listening to the radio
I'm singing "Turn, Turn, Turn";
Help me also to collect and build
and Bridges not to Burn!

Oh Dear God, I beg your help
My heart and soul are twisted and broken;
Please show me a sure sign
of which you are a token.

I need to listen more
the people are out there;
I'm a bit crude and aggressive
Oh please, teach me to care.

Age 44
May 2001

ALL ABOUT OZ

They're off to see the wizard
Who never ate a gizzard;
They didn't encounter a lizard
Nor did they see a blizzard.

The main character was Dorothy
Who in her sleep, did flee;
It started with the poppy
Yet the winding road was key.

She carried a dog named Toto
And he was no dodo;
They never stopped to take a photo
And on the road, was no moto.

They're off to see the wizard
Who never ate a gizzard;
They didn't encounter a lizard
Nor did they see a blizzard.

They wandered upon a Scarecrow
He was clumsy as a newborn doe;
He also could've used some Jo
Rather than take many a blow.

They followed the Yellow Brick Road
Hoping to reach their abode;
With their patience thinning, it showed
They really wanted to explode.

They're off to see the wizard
Who never ate a gizzard;
They didn't encounter a lizard
Nor did they see a blizzard.

They met up with a Tin Man
He couldn't get rusty or tan;
So he carried his oil can
As a decent plan.

They encountered many a fellow
One as mushy as jello;
Most were very mellow
One needed a brain, not a cello.

They're off to see the wizard
Who never ate a gizzard;
They didn't encounter a lizard
Nor did they see a blizzard.

Then there was the Cowardly Lion
He was as mushy as nylon;
He needed to be like Nolan Ryan
Or better, like Monty Python.

They all encountered a witch
One was like a bitch;
When sent thru poppies, they itch
And thus found many a glitch.

Age 45
June 2001

GROWING OLD

As I grow old
I get another cold.
I'm nothing to behold
and I've broken the mold.
Over and over I'm told
I'm starting to fold.

Yes, old at forty-five
and taking a nose-dive.
Daily I push and strive
Just to stay alive.
I no longer thrive
Like a bee in its hive.

I have a sore back
So the bones, the doctor cracks
Then I cough and hack
So energy I lack.
My teeth get more plaque.
Guess it's time to go into the sack.

Age 45
June 2001

DON'T EAT

Don't eat the food
It'll change your mood;
And make you a prude
Remember 'twas made by a brood.

It'll give you pains
And cause you disdain;
So don't eat on the plane
It'll make you go insane.

Don't eat the meat
It's been left in the heat!
Besides, it's rather neat
To dine first at a Blimpie seat.

Just eat your salami
And bring along the baloney,
Buy some fresh coffee
And top off with a candy!

(Enjoy)

Age 45
July 2001

LOCKS OF LOVE

She cuts her hair
For locks of love;
A little girl, neat and rare
Sent from above.

She understands giving
At the tender age of six;
She helps others in living
Who might be in a worse fix.

The locks are made into a wig
For those who have cancer;
Some are small, others big
Because now cancer has no answer.

Yes, you gave locks of love
And some wouldn't dare;
So you became a lovely dove
So others wouldn't stare.

Age 45
July 2001

THE HEAT

We just can't beat
This Lingering Heat.
Up and down the East Coast
We're all starting to roast.
Boston to Raleigh with record highs
And ninety percent letting out sighs.
Forested areas are ablaze
Just from the sun's rays.
No relief is in sight
Though the sun is my delight.
Inside studying with no tan
Don't even need the use of a fan.
But don't complain, next is fall
With wind and rain being the next call.

Age 45
Aug. 2001

REUNION FEARS

The reunion is drawing near
And I'm possessing a lot of fear.
I'm trying to assist
But my fears persist.
Fear abounds in my head
Thinking of what could be said.
My stomach, my face, my eye
I can't even get a guy.
Fear of being talked about
Only makes me sit and pout.

Age 45
Sept. 2001

HOW I MISS

Oh, how I miss my Nuni
And what you meant to me.

How I miss your dresses
And cleaning up the messes.

How I miss us eating out
Going to the city and walking about.

How I miss the garden passes
And meeting me after classes.

How I miss the feasts and fairs
And climbing up the subway's stairs.

How I miss your laugh and smile
And all those created styles.

How I miss your weekend presence
And that awe of maternal elegance.

Age 45
Sept. 2001

IN TIME OF NEED

Tennis, soccer
It doesn't matter;
Baseball, basketball
Cans in every mall—
Everyone's giving proceeds
Even as the market recedes.
Money and blood to give
'Cause we want all to live.
White, Asian, Spanish, Black
Everyone picking up some slack.
Firefighter, EMS or cop
Each went to an assigned stop.
What was Ground Zero
Is now coined "Ground Hero".
Laity, Priests and Ministers
Clergy, nuns and sisters.
Both Yanks and Mets are in action
Proving to be vital distraction.
All children are helping the fund
For they too are stunned.
All are lending a hand
In this vast, vast, land.

Age 45
Sept. 2001

THE MAYOR

I know you don't want praise
I know you don't want adulation;
I know you don't want "Oles"
Or even our "Congratulations".

You're as busy as a bee
Yet taking it in stride;
You've been the major key
Even helping a fatherless bride.

You hold a daily conference
You give widespread updates;
There should be no hindrance
For you're Number One in NY State.

Age 45
Sept. 2001

NEW YORK CITY

New York City
Is such a pity.
People are more humble
As they saw the Towers crumble.
Nothing has been the same
And Bin-Ladin is to blame.
Recently I went down
And saw everyone with a frown.
Downtown is really a mess
I truly must confess.
But everyone is pitching in
Amongst the noise and din.
Money coming from here and there
'cause everyone seems to care.
Donations coming from afar
As Mayor Giulani becomes a star.
Some people still sob
While most return to their job.

Age 45
Oct. 2001

MOTHER MARY

Mother Mary, the Lady in Blue
She'll see you thru
Continue in God's Way
And Mary won't lead you astray.

Mother Mary, the Lady in Blue
Pray to her, when in the pew
Follow on your holy path
And help rid other's wrath.

Mother Mary, the Lady in Blue
In Fatima, with a lovely view
Go to her with your strife
And Mother Mary will ease your life.

Age 45
October 2001

MOTHER MARY (2)

Always follow in God's Ways
And Mother Mary will see you thru.
She'll never lead you astray—
She's Mother Mary—The Lady in Blue.

Go to her with your strife
And Mother Mary will ease your life.
In Fatima—with a lovely view
She's Mother Mary—The Lady in Blue.

Mother Mary—The Lady in Blue.
Watches all, not just a few.
So don't forget to pray
Especially during her month—May.

Continue down God's path
You are headed for a holy bath.
Mother Mary at your side too
Yes Mother Mary—The Lady in Blue.

Age 45
Oct. 2001

A NEW WAR

The war is moving very fast
Causing all faces to be aghast.
Mr. Atef is now past
Causing everyone to have a blast.

Mazar-e-Sharif and Kabul fell
What's next, who can tell?
Little by little we're doing well
If only we can bring Osama to hell.

"No Go" for Ramadan was their pitch
Bush in reply— "Go after every ditch
till we find that lousy witch
that dastardly son of a bitch".

Osama is nowhere to be found
Causing our hands to be bound.
So we will continue to hound
Every hill, cave and mound
Till he is eventually downed!

Age 45
Nov. 2001

THE BOTTLE

The bottle is her curse
The bottle in her purse.

It's always full of liquor
And does the job quicker.

Liquor is slang for booze
And so, all she does is lose.

She likes to drink
And go off the brink.

Whether it's vodka or gin
The situation is a no win.

She starts to attack and vex
This damn bottle is a hex.

Her genre gets very alcoholic
And is no longer Catholic.

Age 45

Wishful Thinking

The Taliban are crumbling
Bin-Laden is on the run;
Yet America's new war
Has really just begun.

We're going from Mazer-e-Sharif
to other sites in Afghanistan;
Now we're being told
This can go to Iraq and Iran.

The newly freed shouted
"Death to the Pakistani";
Then they also shouted
"Death to Omar—the donkey!"

Our troops are on the land and sea
Being in Germany, Turkey, and afar;
Bombs are still exploding
Even in the village of Kandahar.

Geraldo Rivera is reporting
And today almost got shot.
He's in Kandahar
The last major spot.

Earlier atrocities of 30,000
Left one city in a rubble;
So now we are going slow
As not to cause a major fumble.

Some Afghan men decided
To trim their beard;
Breaking a Taliban rule
Which was often feared.

The women on the other hand
Are shedding their turbans;
Pretty soon they'll be
Drinking glasses of bourbon!

Yet others are so joyous
They're collecting booty;
Money, rice and food staples
As if it were a civic duty.

Kids are finally happy
Flying kites in an open sky.
They are finally able
To let out a hearty sigh.

Age 45

YESTERDAY

The world is such a mess
I truly must confess.
War is the reason, I guess
Girls wearing rags instead of a dress
And everyone's spending less.

I long for yesterday—ayer
And at times I have a blank stare.
Nobody really seems to care
Marriage today is rare
And nothing seems fair.

I leave the house each day
Wondering "What will happen today?"
Everyone's walking with dismay
Nobody is happy or gay
So I long for yesterday!

Yesterday was truly better
Everyone being a go getter.
Even though the weather was wetter
I wasn't afraid to open a letter
So now I wish I were an Irish Setter.

Age 45
Nov. 2001

FRIENDSHIP

It was a thrill
to be with you;
Unfortunately I didn't know
what to say, act or do.

It's really hard
to be nice;
When I've always been
like a brick of ice.

Thanks so much
for being my friend;
for I truly hope
I'm on the mend.

Age 45
Nov. 15, 2001

IF OFF TO JAIL

If I went to jail
I wouldn't have bail.
I'd just use my pen
In my cell, eh my den.
I'd write and compose
Rather than bother and impose.
I'd prefer to be alone
Cold and dry like a stone.
I'd write about a future date
Of meeting God at the 'Pearly Gate'.
Then again I may go to hell
Where I'd be in an eternal cell.
I'd write about this or that
Maybe of a sombrero—A Spanish Hat.
So if I went off to jail
I certainly wouldn't fail.

Age 45
Nov. 2001

THANKSGIVING *2001*

Thanksgiving this year was truly a blessing
With all the turkey, food and dressing.
Police and fire crews had to serve
Which gave this day a curve.
Macy's still held their parade
While spirits and dreams didn't fade.
It was seemingly very distinctive
With so many making it so attractive.
A lot more people went to church
To thank God or perhaps to search.

Age 45
Nov. 22, 2001

LARRY RAUSCH

So Larry was a pilot
And the air was his spot.
He loved to fly
And even soar high.
When on a plane, his eyes did glow
As he revved the engine to go.
With his versatility, he saw God
In flight he said a prayer with a nod.
He touched God's hand
As originally planned.
He saw God's face
Amongst the 'Modern Rat Race.'
Because he was truly endowed
Larry is with God floating on a cloud.

Age 45
Nov. 2001

THE OLDIES DANCE

We went to an oldies dance
And on the floor, I took a chance;
He said my makeup did enhance
then he took a stance.

Our stomachs we did nourish
Our friendship's gonna' flourish;
I requested the song "Cherish"
And our feet didn't perish.

The night was warm with no mist,
He held me by my wrist;
We did the Lindy and the Twist
Then we hugged and kissed.

To the main table, we did drift
And there accepted a gift;
Thru the CD's Jerry did sift
And mine wasn't hard to lift.

We thoroughly enjoyed the night
With the background neon light;
It was a pretty sight
And done up just right.

Age 45
Dec. 2001

A PRIEST TO BE

You're training to be a priest
And to celebrate God's feast.
You'll preach about the Trinity
And of Our Lord's mighty Infinity.
You'll learn of His roots—Judaic
Then learn of the Greek icons—mosaic.
You will comprehend Scripture and Gospel
And how the Holy Spirit did dwell.
You'll learn of a city named Galilee
And of Egypt where Jesus had to flee.
Pretty soon, you'll be a deacon
You'll be light—a shining beacon.
You'll be breaking bread
A Sign Jesus rose from the dead.
You'll say, "Take, eat, this is my Body"
For we are all somebody.
Then you'll raise the cup of wine
Another fine, symbolic sign.
You'll say, "Take, this my Blood"
That which Christ shed from the cross of wood.
And you'll learn to do a person's funeral
Which is really their last tribunal.

Age 45
Dec. 20, 2001

Don't and Does

I don't want you
to tell me what to do.
I don't really need
second-hand feed.
All I want is an ear
for someone to hear.
To listen and care
And actually to be there.

I don't want a mom
who's got a mouth like a bomb.
I don't want gifts
That'll cause rifts.
All I want is love
the human type—not from above—
I need someone to care
And go here and there.

Please stop bothering me
Just let me be, let me be.
One day, one day, one day
I'm gonna up and run away.
For I have one, simple command
Won't you just understand.
Yes, I need you to listen and care
Won't you answer this simple prayer?

Age 45
Dec. 2001

MAYOR GIULIANI

Mayor Giuliani—voted man of the year.
Mayor Giuliani—a leader without fear.
Mayor Giuliani—true to the end.
Mayor Giuliani—nerves of steel that don't bend.
Mayor Giuliani—a man of great fortitude
And hence leading the multitudes.
Mayor Giuliani—a man with flair and style.
Mayor Giuliani—leading a bride down the aisle.
Mayor Giuliani—President of the future.
Cause you have healed the sutures.
Mayor Giuliani—going out in style.
Mayor Giuliani—always with a smile.
Mayor Giuliani—meeting victims on the porch.
Mayor Giuliani—even carries the Olympic torch.
Mayor Giuliani—a man full of love and peace.
Mayor Giuliani—a man whose visions never cease.
Mayor Giuliani—a man full of love.
Mayor Giuliani—a leader sent from above.
Mayor Giuliani—genuine to all.
And wouldn't let New York City fall.
Mayor Giuliani—the Chosen One
All in all, a job well done!!
Now without a job, Mayor Giuliani
Perhaps a New York YANKEE.

Age 45
Dec. 2001

MY CAT

I have a cat, Maxine
She's quite funny at night;
She follows my noise and scent
And then follows the light.

At first I try to sleep
But arise to write poetry;
She's funny as she enters
With a mew and a cry.

She encircles the bed
Whacks my face with her tail—
She has to leave her scent
Yes, to leave her trail.

Age 45
Jan. 2002

LOVE

I have a craving, a need
A yearning—It's called Love—
I wish it from my mother and father
Tight fitting like a glove.

I seek to have a lot more
peace of mind and attention;
Less arguing, striking and
of course, less friction.

Love is what it's all about
Cuddling and holding hands;
Eating dinner, watching TV,
Even frolicking in the sand.

A nightly peck on the cheek
A simple, serene kiss;
Leave behind the arguing
Please give me what I miss.

Age 45
Jan. 2002

MOM

My mom just doesn't understand
So I'll stick my head in the sand.
She carries on and can rant and rave
So my room becomes my cave.

I don't seem to get a break
I'd rather jump in a frigid lake.
She goes on and on and on
I'd prefer to be in the john.

She picks and nags
Just like an old hag.
We can't seem to get along
I don't feel as though I belong.

Age 45
Jan. 2002

BUSY, BUSY

When people are busy
It makes me dizzy
And my hair gets frizzy.

They're here and there
And just about everywhere
Everywhere but a chair.

Busy is great for the mind
Not getting in a bind
So it doesn't get behind.

Physically wrenching chores
And things I ignore
Like cleaning the floor.

Shopping, running, playing
With procrastinators delaying
As our hair is graying.

I'll sit and look
And study a book
Do anything but cook.

Eh—forget it
I'd rather sit
Sit, read and knit.

Age 45
Jan. 2002

MY LIFE

My life is tough
So please don't be rough.
Just give me one mo' time
For now I'm in my prime.
I really need a break
To be the frosting on the cake.
Try to be my friend
For I'm at wits end.

Age 45
Jan. 2002

I PRAY

I pray every night
For you to see the light.
I pray every dawn
Not to be on the lawn.
I pray each and every day
That we will have equal say.
I pray every noon
That you'll change soon.
I pray each and every week
That guidance you'll seek.

Age 45
Jan. 2002

MY CAT

My cat shows her contentment
Like a peaceful dove—
She has a temperament
And came from heav'n above.

She rubs and caresses
After running thru the hall.
She jumps, kneads and presses
Then rolls into a ball.

She stays on mom's lap
She lays by dad.
She loves to catnap
Any soft spot is her pad.

She ascends her throne
Which is really my bed.
She is affection prone
Then rolls and plays dead.

She's quite a gem
Just like cultured pearls,
Her tail is her stem
For her body she'll curl.

Age 45
Jan. 2002

THE GOLDEN GIRL

Sarah, you won the gold
At just sixteen years old.
To me you're a gem; a diamond
Because I'm so very, very fond.
I was truly, truly happy
When you skated so flawlessly.
I prayed & prayed & prayed
That the judging wouldn't go astray.
For you have got the best style
And the cutest little smile.
I'm sure you made your parents proud
As well as everyone in the crowd.
So our new idol is Sarah Hughes
Who just made the Headline News.
As a finale, you did a lovely tribute
Our brethren, you did salute.
You skated to "You'll Never Walk Alone"
For into our hearts you have flown.

Age 45
February 2002

DIFFICULT

I find it rather difficult
To listen to and obey you;
Its truly hard at my age
To follow what you say or do.

We have to give and take
It's a game of fifty-fifty;
Then all our lives would
Seem a bit more nifty.

You don't give leeway
You're a female Stalin;
Sometimes I even think
You could pass for Lenin.

Setting thousands of rules
Won't make me change;
In fact it'll only make
Me act more strange!

About your list of rules—
You have to draw the line;
And then I'll start
To act just fine.

Give it a try and see
Let me roam free;
Let me be carefree
I wanna be me.

Age 45
Feb. 2002

MY RADIO

My little pink radio
is my friend;
It doesn't nag or pick
Neither does it OFFEND!

It never, ever
does me wrong;
It just plays
another neat song!

It soothes and plays
some really nice tunes;
I'll calm down as
Frank Sinatra croons.

It doesn't answer back
Even if I get real angry,;
It'll try to soothe me
For it's a friend—you see.

Age 45
Feb 2002

Diverse America

I watched Ted Koppel's "Town Hall"
It was like being in a Mega-Mall.
All types of boutiques, shops and stores
With various people exiting from the doors.
Each represented a different place
Each being of a different race.
Some were yellow, Chinese and Japanese
Afghani, Americans talked of the detainees.
Cubans talked about green cards
And then all talked about guards.
All shapes and colors were represented
And this night, all problems presented.
At times they argued pro and con
Yet wishing all evil had gone.
They talked of screenings and freedom
All this due to four bombs.

Age 45
March 2002

YIELDING

I have to stop the buts
I can't always be justified,
I need to live in God's Path
So help me to be purified.

Age 45
March 2002

HUMILITY

Oh God, allow me to be humble
Please let my philosophy tumble.
For in Your Path and Way
I've lingered and gone astray.

Teach me not to stumble
Nor stupidity to mumble.
Let this be a new day
Oh Gad, let me start today.

Allow my heart to melt and crumble
Allow me to go straight and not fumble.
So please, teach me to obey
And make me do as You Say.

Age 45
March 2002

THE RAIN AT LAST

The reservoir looks like a desert
Showing us less water, yet more sand.
Alas, the rains have finally come
To this parched, arid—laden land.
So we have a wee bit of rain
But it barely did any good.
Yet the storm that we had
So fierce, everyone needed a hood.
Indeed, we really got this rain
Late last night, it poured and poured.
People were wet and cars skidding
But yet our prayers were answered by the Lord.

Amen

Age 45
March 2002

IT'S EASTER!

Yes, Yes it's Easter!

E—in Easter is for the Eggs.
A—in Easter is Jesus' Arrival.
ST—in Easter is for the Spring Time.
E—in Easter is for Eternal Glory.
R—in Easter is for the Risen Christ.

So it's Easter, let us Rejoice!

Rejoice? YES Spring is in the air,
Flowers budding, Lilies in Full Bloom.

Rejoice? **YES** *indeed—a*
New birth—a new beginning.

So out with the old
Bring in the New—
Bring in Easter Week.

Age 45
March 2002

A NEW FRIEND

I'm in the hospital
Which isn't very fun;
I'm rooming with a girl
Who is like a semi-nun.

She is also Catholic
And prays a lot too;
Then she cheers me up
When I seem blue.

I guess the good Lord
Sent her to me;
So I gotta be a friend
As one should be.

I'm sure she is
Taking Jeanne's place;
So I thank the Lord
If that be the case.

Age 45
March 2002

GIVING OF MYSELF

I shouldn't really take
clothes that one brings;
Where poverty surrounds me
and no-one ever sings.

They'll gladly accept it
And a heck of a lot more;
They'll smile and accept me
With open arms at the door.

I have to truly learn
to give treasures away;
What I truly want
even if it doesn't fray.

These are no second hands
or hand me downs;
They're brand new
and not meant for clowns.

The sweats are real
pretty-just a tad big;
Mom said she'd hem
To fit my legs like a twig.

Yet I yearn to
fill a deep bag;
'cause some elderly
clothes really sag.

Age 45
April 2002

RESPECT

Respect is a pretty song
Yet its' contents—to get along.

R is naturally for Respect
E is not for some—but Everyone
S is for Showing and Sharing it
P is for other people!
E is to the Elderly
C is to the Children
T is for Totally and Timely.

So wake up and
Show some RESPECT
Not only today
But each and everyday.

Age 45
April 2002

MEANING OF THE CROSS

Each and everyone
Has a cross to bear;
I guess for sinning
That is our fare.

For some it's heavy
For others light;
So for our sinning
The cross is our plight.

No matter what
We have to carry it;
For God truly knows
Which size will fit.

For Adam did sin
Now we have to fight;
For a place in heaven
Which will be our delight.

Don't make any mistakes
To see God's wrath;
Then Heav'n will be waiting
If we choose God's Path.

Age45
April 2002

RESPECT

R *is for Respecting Me*

E *is for Eternity*

S *is for Show me*

P *is for living Peacefully*

C *is do it Carefully*

T *is Treat Me Tactfully*

Please show me Respect
And we'll get along
Otherwise you can
Forget that nice song.

Age 45
April 2002

THE LORD VS. ME

I took varied pills
Yet he wanted me to live
In a roundabout way
He said "Life was to give".

I jumped in front of a car
He still wanted me to live
I guess the Lord God
Wanted me to forgive.

He sends troubles along the way
He wants me very much alive
I know God doesn't want
Me to take another nose-dive.

It's the 'Road Not Taken'
Each and everyday
I'm sure the Lord God
Is waiting for me to obey.

Age 45
April 2002

LONELY

I am ever
so lonely
Like the last single
Leaf on a tree.

As you can
easily see
I'm never with
Two or three.

All I do is
weep and cry
And at times
want to die.

I want to tell the
world good-bye
Because no one ever
says "Hello or HI".

I've made my bed
In it, I have to lie
I lay there still
And let out a sigh.

Life is real tough
You can easily see
So now I'm paying
A dastardly fee.

I have no one
to call my friend
I'm really at
My wit's end.

My forlorn spirit
Is like tattered rags
And like a angry dog
My tail no longer wags.

Age 46

A TRIBUTE TO GRANDMA

My Grandma, Nuni, was the best,
She was so full of vim, vigor and zest.

Her heart was always warm,
Amidst many a worldly storm.

She tried to help everyone,
And was truly so much fun.

She loved to sew, chat and dance,
And many lives grandma did enhance.

When needed, she was always there,
For she always seemed to care.

With all her goodness and smiling face,
She is now in God's heavenly resting place.

Age 46
Aug. 2002

SCHOOL TODAY

Murder and shootings
Bodies lying still
Boys using violence
setting out to kill.

Teachers blaming society
then turning away
While the grief
lingers and stays.

Yet the teenage girls
use counter pills
Using a quick fix
To end earthly bills.

Parents involved
in many a melee
So their kids
are going astray.

Age 46
Aug. 2002

GOOD LIFE

I love my wife
I love my life
I play a fife
So I have no strife
And rarely use a knife.

Life is very neat
In the dry heat
Where two lovers meet
In an acrid field of wheat
Then kiss in the back seat.

Dreams can become true
Between me and you
If we say and do
And perform like glue
For I always knew.

One day we'd be in a pew
Taking a wink as a cue
Or possibly a clue
As to never being blue
Nor having to stew.

So strike up the band
For life can be grand
It doesn't have to be bland
If you romp in the sand
Then wrestle on dry land.

Age 46
Aug. 2002

AT LOSS

Without my precious Nuni
I can no longer go
Down to Little Italy
For the Feast of San Gennaro.
She always bought me cannoli
But death became her foe;
Again I ask why
Why did she have to die?
She died a horrible death
With Alzheimer's at the door;
It took her last breath
Which we could not ignore.
She breathed her last sigh
Oh why did she have to die?

Age 46
Sept. 2002

POETRY

Poetry is my thing
As the words begin to ring.
Like a thick lotion
My pen goes in motion.
Every three or four hours
Words will come like showers.
They are a dictionary's tower
Hence language shows its power.
Some fall here, some there
On the paper from the air.
For my brain's always working
And ideas are lurking.
So I love to rhyme
Each and every single time.
There is varied poetry
In each and every society.
There's prose, poetry and verse
None of which is terse.
From Japan comes haiku
Syllables are just a few.
From England comes the sonnet
Just a pretty as a bonnet.
If I try for a book entry
It's serious and non-elementary.
So I try my very best
To win that yearly contest.

Age 46

POETRY IN SONG

For the Rolling Stones' "Satisfaction"
There is still a lot of dedication.

Also for the Beatles' "Yesterday"
Which we hear home and away.

Equally famous "All You Need Is Love"
Not only by siblings, but also from above.

We often listen to "In The Mood"
It'll make you happy, not brood.

There's "Bad, Bad Leroy Brown"
Which is heard throughout the town.

Johnny Cash does "A Boy Named Sue"
I wish I knew his point of view.

Sammy Davis sang "The Candy Man"
For a sweet melody was his plan.

Cubby Checker sings and does "The Twist"
While everyone else stomped and kissed.

There's Elvis' "Love Me Tender"
Especially for the female gender.

Then there's the party song "Shout"
Which is what it's all about.

In the summer there's "Surfin USA"
Which to me is surely O-K.

A prom favorite is "Cherish"
So popular, this tune will never perish.

Neil Sedaka chimed in "Sweet Caroline"
Which is a favorite of mine.

Another favorite is "Leavin' On A Jet Plane"
For it is better than a stuffy train.

Ol Blue Eyes croons "New York, New York"
As we dine on sweet and sour pork.

Another travel song is "Going To Kansas City"
But if I go, it'll be such a pity.

Don McClean sang "American Pie"
While my thoughts truly soared high.

There's "Song So Blue"
Hoping it's only for one or two.

I'd rather hear "Don't Worry, Be Happy"
For it's such an upbeat melody.

A pretty ballad is "Precious and Few"
Meant for just the two of you.

Age 46
Sept. 2002

IN HONOR

Many boats set sail
And their anchors didn't fail!
They came from around the globe
While investigators continue to probe.
It was a splendid day
As they left New York Bay.
They sailed up the Hudson waters
In respect for those slaughtered.
They paid a lovely tribute
For their mission was to salute.
For a year has passed by
Yet the citizens still cry.
In the river lay roses
For history never closes.
Now we all hope for peace
And pray that war and terror may cease.

Age 46
Sept. 2002

LONELINESS

I've nowhere to go
And nowhere to hide.
I've no-one to talk to
And in no-one do I confide.
I'm in such a mess
And oh—so alone
That all my conversation
Is done over the phone.
I don't look forward
To the following day
I only just wish
I were Far, Far Away.

Age 46
Sept. 2002

LIFE'S FEARS

It's awfully sad to say
Life is just another day.
Terrorists taunt and kill
And then bodies lie still.
Most awake frightened
From alerts being heightened.
There are missiles and bombs
Killing dads and moms.
So there is talk of an attack
On Saddam Hussein and Iraq.
War continues to rage
To put him in his cage.
Colin Powell is on the go
Trying to make friend from foe.
Each nation holds some blame
Yet no one has any shame.
Now we need a lot of help
Just like a little puppy's yelp.
We also have to follows God's word
And leave behind the devil's Sword.
What is needed is true peace
So that war may cease.

Captured Dec 13, 2003

Age 46
August 2002

OCTOBER

October brings descending leaves
Fall, cool breezes and other changes;
Layered clothes and
Snow on the mountain ranges.

Geese fly south
Temps drop;
Shops hold sales
Making people shop.

Children settled in school
Chores replacing playtime;
There's a new set of rules
No play until bells chime.

There are parades
for Columbus Day;
people leave early
without any delay.

Leaves fall and turn
They lose their hue;
Which gives the Palisades
A very rustic view.

Autumn marches on
Soon it'll be Halloween;
With dragons and beast
Each girl can be a queen.

Children ring bells
for 'Trick or Treat'
Hoping for something
really, really sweet.

Age 46
Sept. 18, 2002

WELLINGTON HALL

Wellington Hall is the center for care
And where the nurses are fair.
The nursing manager is Josie
Whose attitude is always rosy.
All the staff have warm smiles
And they dress with classy styles.
But don't use the call bell often
For then they will harden, not soften.
Every day they make your bed
Change the linens and fix the spread.
Each room is equipped with cable
And their pet rabbit is as soft as sable.
They even have a whirlpool
Which is so neat and cool.
Every day there's hourly therapy
To lead you on the road to recovery.
The activities director is Nadine
Who is very happy and serene.
Her co-worker is Randy
Who is sweet as candy.
The other aide is Luz
Who never blows her fuse.
Each day brings a different event
That I wish there were a room for rent.
Every Monday there is a Mass
Which no Catholic should bypass.
Every Friday there's Happy Hour
With lots of sweets and nothing sour.
A bingo win pays a dime
Each and every single time.
There's Name That Tune and Sing-a-Long
With lot of music and guess that song.
The food has a great taste
And nothing is made in haste.
So one can truly see
This is the place to be.

Age 46
Sept. 2002

ANGELS SONG

The angels passed by
While dropping from the sky.
We were truly endowed
As they came from the cloud.
They came down to earth
To give us new birth.
They bestowed God's grace
Upon the whole human race.
They said, "Don't act in haste
And always try to be chaste".
They also implored, "Lead a good life
Even in these times of hate and strife".
So God showed His might
Through this Celestial sight.
This was God's majestic plan
From simple tribe to large clan.
For it's plain to see
We should live in harmony.

Age 46
Sept. 2002

"YA GOTTA BELIEVE"

It's the story of 'YA GOTTA BELIEVE'
With the case of Christopher Reeve.
He has long come to realize
He'll get better with exercise.
He's getting his strength back
By exercising on a stationary tract.
He now moves his legs and fingers
That he won't let his recovery linger.
Then he pedals away on his bike
Demonstrating his mammoth psyche.
Reeve is earnestly looking to get better
Because he is a true go-getter.
He has turned activist from actor
Which has been a key factor.
Reeve is desperately seeking a cure
That modern science can't ignore.
So he recently appeared on 'Donahue'
To share his point of view.

Age 46
Sept. 2002

MY KITTY CAT

I hear a pitter-patter
of my little cats feet
Except for when the
weather turns to sleet.

Then he will truly
slip and slide
Down the sidewalk
He will glide.

His cushiony paws
will turn ever so cold
So in my arms
The cat I will hold.

I'll then place him
on my warm lap
Where he'll snooze
and take a nap.

Later on we'll retreat
into my soft bed
He'll spend the night
at the foot of the spread.

He'll lie contented
and start to purr
As I rub and pet
His soft bodily fur.

Age 46
Oct. 2002

SENATOR TORRICELLI

Senator Torricelli once had fame
He also had a lot of clout;
Now he hangs his head in shame
And he's also down and out.

He did favors for Mr. Chang
But it brought him bad news;
It has gnarled like a fang
Bringing Torricelli the blues.

He lied and cheated
That he burst his bubble;
He is now defeated
With his life turned to rubble.

Most say he has to pay the price
Others have used the word "Resign"
Whichever way we roll the dice
He may even have to pay a fine.

With a month left he quit
His deception brought him down;
Seems as though he lied a bit
Therefore he retreats to his hometown.

So he's leaving the political race
His career seems to be over;
Torricelli has abandoned his place
For he's going to be a lost rover.

His reputation is tumbling
His wheeling and dealing were the worst;
His popularity is quickly crumbling
And his personal wounds need to be nursed.

Age 46
Oct. 2002

WHAT IS THANKSGIVING

Thanksgiving need not be a special day
Especially when nice people come your way.

Thanksgiving is knowing people like you
Thanksgiving is for the niceties you do.

Thanksgiving is for going that extra mile
And for showing your customers that ever ready smile.

Thanksgiving is for people who truly care
Because people like you are so very rare.

Thanksgiving is for people that do so much
And for those that add the finishing touch.

Thanksgiving is for people who like to please
And that their smile reaches over the seas.

Thanksgiving comes back for giving from the heart
And knowing your attitude is sweet and not tart.

People like you are few and far between
So remember this Thanksgiving you're a queen.

Age 46
Nov. 2002

FROM THE HEART

I really want to be your friend
And our relationship we have to mend.
I know you've shed many a tear
So let me make my case very clear.
I know I don't always try hard
And I should play by your card.
But please, oh please try to bend
Because I'm at my wit's end.

I know I caused a lot of aggravation
And don't give you much satisfaction.
You claim that I don't measure up
And at times I tend to disrupt.
Just realize that I had a rough life
Full of anger, turmoil and strife.
So I need a hand which you can lend
Yes, I need a mom that I can depend.

You see my life is very difficult
Compared to that of a lightening bolt.
Being struck, beaten and defeated
Hence my nerve system is heated.
So please try to really understand
That all my actions aren't planned.
So please. Oh please your patience lend
And patiently try to be my friend.

Age 46
Nov. 2002

TAKE TIME

Take time to smell the roses
But don't thumb up your noses.
Take time to enjoy God's beauty
For it is your civic and moral duty.
Take time to help others
Strangers, parents, sisters and brothers.
Again take time to be extra kind
For you'll take a load off your mind.
Take time to enjoy a tasty treat
Whether in the cold or in the heat.
Take extra time to enjoy the moment
While you sit still and lay dormant.

Age 46
Nov. 2002

DEAR JOHN:

I've grown numb
I feel like a crumb.
I don't know what to do
Except to listen to you.
I don't know what to say
All I can do is pray.
I listened and learned
Then went home concerned.
What has gone wrong
Why do you sing such a sad song?
Oh Dear John,
What are you on?
Are you on a binge—
You seem to be on the fringe.
Are you on booze
Trying to blow a fuse?
Are you doing drugs
Instead of getting hugs?
So please listen to me
And go for some therapy.
I don't know what type
But John, the time is ripe.
Please come to your senses
And conquer those thorny fences.
For I am full of worry
So please get help in a hurry.
Please break your silence
For I'm losing my patience.
And if you need help
Just give a quick yelp.
For John, please be aware
That I indeed, really do care.

Age 47
Dec. 2002

THE FIRST SNOW

The first snow of the year
Is really in full gear.
Six inches seemed to be enough
Making the going rough and tough.

Cars seemed to be slipping
And sliding all over the place;
With black ice on the road
Considerably slowing the pace.

The south had a worst storm
And it took a different form.
Wires and trees laden the ice
Causes outages to many a device.

Age 46
Nov 2002

MOTHER TERESA

Mother Teresa was a beloved nun
Found toiling and laboring in the torrid sun.
Often referred to as Saint of the Gutter
Never a negative word did she utter.
She travelled from east to west
Doing her work with so much zest.
Mother Teresa did many a task
And obeyed each Pontiff as asked.
She was sent from heaven above
To bestow upon us God's Love.
She would never, ever ignore
Doing her utmost for the poor.
It was truly her earnest will
To care for the abandoned and ill.
Although diminutive in size
She won the Nobel Peace Prize.
When accepting the award, she was humbled,
And throughout her pious life, never stumbled.
Mother Teresa was so down to earth
Showing one what life was really worth.
A former Pontiff gave her a car
Which she didn't use very far.
She said her feet would suffice
As she gave out bowls and staples of rice.
Mother Teresa was very modest
And you couldn't find a person more honest.
So it's an honor for the Pope to beatify
For many Catholics' he'll truly satisfy.

Age 47
Jan. 2003

2003

We rang in the year
With a lot of good cheer.
And as we faithfully danced
The night was enhanced.
Everyone is praying for peace
Noting that the wars should cease.
Yet flaws got in the way
As we continued to pray.
A baby was to be cloned
And Catholics decidedly moaned.
Early on, six inches of snow fell
Making the morning commute hell.
The conjoined twins finally went to their abode
Yet their progress has markedly slowed.
They will need follow up care
As others pay their airfare.
Newark Children were found neglected
And now they are being protected.
Church statues are being vandalized
As war preparations, being finalized.
All this in a few short weeks
Yet peace is what one seeks.

Age 47
Jan. 2003

HAPPY BIRTHDAY

Happy Birthday to a special friend
Hoping the friendship won't soon end.
Jerry, you simply deserve the best
And you'll always be the robin in my nest.
Eh, whad'ya say—age fifty six
Now's the time to get your kicks!
So here's hoping all will go well
Cause you are a guy who is swell.
I hope you have a blessed day
With great things coming your way.

Age 47
Jan. 2003

WHO

Peter or Jerry
Who shall it be?
I pray to God
That He will guide me.

Jerry is reticent
Peter is a bit mature;
Which of the two
I'm not too sure.

Friday I saw Peter
Saturday 'twas Jerry.
Both of the nights were
As sweet as cherry.

With Jerry—Leonia Café
With Peter—The Plaza Diner.
So eating out
Could not be finer.

Age 47
Jan. 2003

FR. RONALD GRAY

All the parishioners are brokenhearted
That Fr. Ron has departed.
He was a simple yet feisty priest
Who celebrated the Mass as a major feast.
Born in Chicago as Francis Joseph Gray,
He decided to follow the Lord and obey.
Fr. Gray was loving and warm,
To him many people did swarm.
He was assigned to St. Cecilia's Priory
Because he was outgoing, yet fiery.
He later became a pastor
Only to serve the Lord as his Master.
He then came to St. John's
Affectionately known as "Father Ron".
He believed in little acts of kindness,
And to our sins he'd show blindness.
He held steadfast to the Little Flower
Who had ideals as high as a tower.
Father liked to preach this "Little Way of Perfection".
And he'd say "DO THIS IN MEMORY OF ME"
with reflection.
Father was known for his eloquent preaching
Yet his warm smile was very far reaching.
Father Ron was active to the end,
For his faith he wanted to defend.
He left this world in style
Leaving behind a "Gigantic Smile".

Age 47
Feb. 2003

TRIBUTE TO COLUMBIA

Seven lovely, smiling faces
All coming from various places.
Israel gave us Ilan Ramon
Who never had a face of stone.
From Virginia came David Brown
Who never seemed to frown.
From Texas came Vic Husband
His life seemed to be so grand.
From Washington, there was Michael Anderson
Who as a father had so much fun.
From Wisconsin, there came Laurel Clark
Her smile lit her face like a spark.
From California came Willie McCool
Who was very smart and not a fool.
India sent us friendly Kalpana Chawla
Who would have loved a homecoming gala.
So near and yet so far
Now each is a shining star.

Age 47
Feb. 2003

MY FRIEND JERRY

My friend Jerry, is one of a kind
Always having kindness on the mind.
He's not a tiger, but a gentle Ben
Who protects you as if in a den.
With regularity he calls
He's not one to climb walls.
Along with a listening ear
These calls bring a lot of cheer.
Jerry always goes the extra mile
And he always comes with the Eveready Smile.
With him, you'll never feel neglected
Not even rejected nor dejected.
For Jerry is so full of compassion
As he demonstrates niceness that is in fashion.
So I must simply and truthfully attest
That my friend Jerry is the very best.

Age 47
March 2003

FRIENDS

Do you need a friend
Till the very end?
I certainly do
Especially when I am blue.

I need someone's shoulder
As big and tall as a boulder,
To cushion my fears
And ease my wet tears.

One such friend is Jerry
Who always tries to be merry.
He lends a listening ear
And his phone calls always bring me cheer.

Another lady friend is Mary
Whose views never vary.
She is always sweet and kind
Especially if you are in a bind.

Age 47
March 2003

EXERCISE

Spring is the time for exercise
It's time for the wise
To forgo their fries.

Time to lose pounds
Time to make rounds
With nature and musical sounds.

Exercise can be knee bends
Down, down as the body descends.

It can consist of push-ups
And time to discontinue the syrups.

You can also partake of jumpin' jacks
To fit into your new slacks.

Ten minutes on the treadmill
Will keep you anything but still.

You can jog in place
But keep a steady pace.

Age 47
April 2003

A SAD DAY

There was a bride
And also a groom.
They each died
In a fit of gloom.

They were to be husband
And also wife.
But he didn't understand
Which led to strife.

There should have been pride
Instead of total doom.
Their vows took a slide
As she was shot in the room.

So much for the wedding band
Instead he took a life.
He never held her hand
But used a gun rather than a knife.

Age 47
May 2003

WAR

Is there another war
Knocking at our door?
Bush spoke of compassion
And that it's still in fashion.
Yet are we prepared to go
To fight against the foe?
Will we go after Saddam
Like a bear or a ram?
It seems to be getting tense
As we near the enemy's fence.

Age 47
May 2003

* Captured December 13, 2003

THE NJ DEVILS

While the fans roar
The New Jersey Devils score.
The cup is back
Right on track.
They won in Game Seven
With everyone screaming to high Heaven.
There was a giant street fiesta
And no-one acted like a jester.
Screams, yells and shouts
Were heard all about.
You win a prize
of enormous, gigantic size.
Such is the case
of being First Place.

Age 47
May 2003

ANGELS

Angels here, Angels there
Angles over and above my hair.
They wear a halo of gold
And help us to join God's fold.
Our guardian angel watches over us
Such is the case while in car or bus.
Some have a human touch
When they care so much.
Such is the case of Jerry
Who is as sweet as a cherry.
Another angel is Mary
Whose faith doesn't wary.

Age 47
May 2003

THE FACE OF DEPRESSION

You always feel down
And you wear a frown.
You start to cry
At times, you want to die.
You're in bed in May
Each and every day.
Everything bothers you
Even the kindness of a few.
You drag and can't get up
Agony fills your cup.
Others around you are happy
While you feel real crappy.
Life is less than fun
So you continue to run.
Everything you do is uphill
And nothing is a thrill.
You no longer pray or eat
Life marches to a different beat.
Every day is a struggle
Your needs you can no longer juggle.
Such is the face of depression
That you live life with apprehension.

Age 47
May 2003

OUR FAILING PONTIFF

John Paul is ready for his Judgment Day
For he feels the Lord he did obey.
He is content to leave this earth
For all that which it is worth.
J. P. II always offered a ray of hope
As he was our long reigning pope.
Although he has a heart of gold
We must admit the Pontiff is getting old.
Unfortunately, he's gotten sickly and ill
But this, too, could be God's Will.
I still ask that never-ending "WHY?"
As we head for a futuristic GOOD-BYE.

Age 47
May 2003

MY CANADIAN TRIP

After meeting me in the airport
Diane gave me food for thought.
She laid out many a plan
While driving home in a van.
She spoke of a few varied errands
Some of which I cannot stand.
She had a good idea for t'morrow
Which won't bring me any sorrow.
For June 11ᵗʰ is my birthday
And I'll have most of the say.
She and I, and friends are going out to eat
I don't care if it's fish or meat.
Although Diane didn't bake
She bought me a lovely chocolate cake.
On it was written 'Happy Birthday Doreen'
Oh my God, I simply feel like a Queen.
She showed me pix of yesteryear
Which brought to my eye, many a tear.
My original visit was World Youth Day
When we were happy and gay.
When out on an errand I bought Di a rose
For all her compassion and kindness that flows.
She is so understanding and kind
That people like Diane are hard to find.
On Thursday I'll be with Aileen
Whose attitude is very serene.
Aileen is taking me to gamble
Hoping my money won't be in a shamble.
Next up is a trip to Cumbermere
A place which is a tad far, not near.
It's noted for its famed 'Madonna House'
If weather permits, I'll wear a pretty blouse.
For our trip, Fr. Ken had a good plan
He offered us the use of his van.
We stopped on the way to eat
Most of us having fish, not meat.
I had a plate of garlicky shrimp
That Wilf, with his jokes, was an imp.

The weather was chilling to the bone
No weather even for an ice cream cone.
After arriving there, we had a tour
For we were five, not four.
Around five we had a healing mass
After passing through the soggy grass.
They blessed my head and hands with oil
After I saw the community toil.
Unfortunately it rained all day
Even as we knelt down to pray.
Over dinner we exchanged tales
For true friendship never fails.
Although I didn't visit a steeple
I was in the midst of friendly people.
Saturday was day of much needed rest
And the weather was at its absolutely best.
It got so warm I had to remove my sweater
Now this day and time couldn't get much better.
We drove about here and there
In the NICE, FRESH AIR.
48 hours and it's time to go
I hope the time passes slow.
For Saturday night I suggested a picnic
She agreed—the hot dogs were quick.
We also had my Macaroni Salad and a pickle
For once in my life, I wasn't fickle.
On Sunday after Mass, there's a birthday party
For an elderly lady who was very hearty.
A young lady in the parish died
Which disrupted the serene tide.
My trip is surely winding down
Gosh, I'm sure gonna' miss this town.
She even rooted for the Nets to do their best
Knowing she had an American as her special guest.
I'll certainly have a tear in my eye
When I have to say my final "Good-Bye".
This is perhaps my longest poem
The next one will come from Rome.

Age 47
June 2003

POETIC PLANETS

We will have begun
After the rising sun.

First up comes Mercury
Which could carry some curry.

There is fiery Venus
So hot, it'll clear your sinus.

Then we have our own planet Earth
Still having discrepancies of its birth.

One farther out is Mars
Which didn't invent Hershey Bars.

Next over there's Jupiter
Which doesn't have a monitor.

With flashing rings there is Saturn
They sure are pretty and don't burn.

Still further we come upon Uranus
Which is probably solid and porous.

We then come across Neptune
Which can't come up too soon.

Last ad infinitum comes Pluto
At the end of our galaxy, finito.

Age 47
June 2003

LIFE

Life is so very short
So sing, sing, sing;
As does the happy King
In his royal court.

Learn things that are taught
For life is not a fling;
It should be treated like a ring
So don't bicker for naught.

Precious life we shouldn't abort
But to it we should cling;
For a babe has so much to bring
And good lessons are sought.

Age 47
June 2003

LIFE'S PHILOSOPHY

Exercise
When you rise—

Dress
For success;

Eat
A lot of wheat—

Savor
The flavor.

Read
To succeed—

Learn
To earn;

Create
Don't deviate—

Beautify
To satisfy.

Pray
Each and every day—

Then Rest
To be your best;

But Fight
For your right.

Age 47
July 2003

JERRY AND I

Jerry and I shared some intimate views
And he gave me some good news.
He said, "In the future I might care for you
And then choose you to be my beau".
We talked further of our mutual interests
And how we're the straw in each others' nests.
He is always there for me
His internal caring I can truly see.
He is like a royal King
Always presenting me with something.
He apologizes if he decides to holler
And doesn't treat me like a dog on a collar.
Rather Jerry tries to use a lot of respect
Even if I'm rude or decide to interject.

Age 47
August 2003

THE WORST BLACKOUT

August '03 brought us a blackout
But no-one seemed to shout.
It hit up and down the East Coast
With major cities being black like toast.
It seemed that most of the power
Was leaving every central tower.
Dairy and produce spoiled and went bad
As restaurateurs grew angry and sad.
So everything came to a screeching halt
And this time, terror was not at fault.
People decided to help each other
Whether stranger, neighbor or brother.
It was just instinctive reaction
That most jumped into action.
Some decided to direct traffic
So others, mainly elders wouldn't panic.
People returned to the old fashioned porch
Occasionally using the flashlight as a torch.
Strangers A and B soon became friends
While even the races made amends.
With a situation like this, it never fails
That lots of folks exchanged wild tales.
After being tired, a lot slept in Central Park
Gathering at mid day—dusk and finally dark.

Age 47
Aug. 2003

GAMBLING AT THE STRIP

Gambling can be fun
Especially if you are up and have won.
The best payoff is the Showboat
So this casino gets my vote.
Another nice one is the Claridge
Which is appropos for love and marriage.
Down over at Bally's
Your money really tallies.
Further away you'll find the 'Trump'
Which is certainly no dump.
There is also the Taj Mahal
Meant for you and your gal.
Speaking of the Taj
Won't bring to mind the Haj.
Of course you can stay at the Hilton
But it won't have a convention about Milton.
A smaller one is the Sands
Yet it still deals a lot of hands.
The newest casino is the Borgata
I bet it even serves Horchata.

Age 47
August 2003

GAMBLING

Gambling can be so much fun
Until you're dry and the money's done.
There is Blackjack and the Wheel
Or you can go where they deal.
You can have a round of craps
Then finish by eating Turkey Wraps.
Maybe your thing is poker
Especially with the added joker.
You can get an easy straight
With the wild deuce as bait.
The machines have 'double down'
I'll have a heck of a time on the town.
There is also another game—Five Card Stud
I hope it doesn't leave you in the mud.
Some machines even use nickels
So the elderly won't get into a pickle.
Mainly however, most play quarters
And while playing you can get water.
You can always take a reprieve on the boardwalk
Where the pigeons, crows and birds stalk.
Some go out to get rays of sun
Before returning to hit for 'twenty-one'.
There's even a game called Keno
Here in Atlantic City, not just Reno.
Play the cards and you'll get a comp
As back to A.C. next month you'll romp.
If you win it won't be a curse
So if a woman, you can buy a purse.
As you can tell, gambling is wild
And certainly not meant for a child.

Age 47
Aug. 2003

A NEW NIGHTGOWN

I no longer have an ugly, long frown
For I bought a pretty purple nightgown.
Mom picked it out
As I looked all about.
We looked on every rack
As I tried to keep track.
It has flowers and butterflies
And it's just my perfect size.
It even has a pretty pocket
A tad small for a locket.
It feels great for TV
As one can truly see.
It's so airy and comfy as I lay in bed
Even if I'm on top of the spread.
And one cannot fail
By getting it on sale.

Age 47
Aug. 2003

POETIC CREATIVITY

Pen, Paper are my thing
Can't you just tell
For words and poetry
Hath cast a mighty spell.

So don't bother me
As I sit and write
In fact, I'd rather have
You out of my sight.

I write alone in my room
in peace and tranquility
As I touch base with nature
weather, food and even morality.

I've written 'bout religious
About grandma and mothers
I've done a lot about cats
As well as idols and others.

So leave me in peace
and let me stay free
For I've a pen in hand
To create poetry, you see.

Age 47
Aug 2003

A PRAYER

O Dear God, You know what I think and what I do
So Dear God, this day I ask You to be true.

It's a mad competition, you well know
So let me try to go with the flow.

O Dear God, please be my guide
See me through, for in Thee I confide.

Allow me to take this with a grain of salt
Unscramble my mind and let me come to a peaceful halt.

Only you know what is best for me
So let me see this competition with clarity.

If it is meant for me to win
Let me not be greedy and fall into sin.

I'd like to win, this is for sure
For my verse speaks volumes and the words roar.

I'd spend some publishing to spread your Word
Your Word in poetry and verse which should be heard.

So lastly I ask you to be fair
And give me a cross that I can bear.

So again I ask you to be my Guide
And please don't hurt my pride.

Age 47
August 2003

A RARE SWIM

After many years, I went for a swim
It was during a convention and not at the gym.
I decided to try more than one lap
And afterwards, I really needed a bathing cap.
I swam and even did the side stroke
But later on I was sore and needed a warm soak.
After a few laps I needed some rest
For my body is not at its' best.
I then realized I'm not in shape
When by midnight my body started to ache.
Three days later I was at it again
This time instead of five I did ten.
All in all, I guess the practice was good
Even though my muscles feel like wood.
Practice makes perfect—they say
I guess I'll get it right someday.

Age 47
Aug. 2003

WHAT IS

What is success?
Is it an abundance of health?
Is it monetary and worldly wealth?
Is it being able to process
An amount of intelligence?

What is happiness?
Is it the eternal, everlasting joy
Of birthing a newborn, baby boy?
Is it a measure of kindness?
For me, it's more, it's true faithfulness.

What is love?
Does it come from your mother?
Or perhaps from another?
I know it cometh from the Father above
Who treats one with a kid glove.

Success, Happiness and Love
Is in finding God
It's giving Him a true nod
Acknowledging the Trinity, the Dove
And knowing God reigns above.

Age 47
Sept. 2003

ANGER

You make my blood boil
As I become like a snake that'll coil.
Everyday another stupid question or comment
Daily, hourly or at any moment.
I clench my teeth and seethe
At times I don't want to breathe.
You look to pick a fight
So then I decide to spite.
You pry into my personal life
You're causing me a lot of strife.
I don't do alcohol or drugs
But now I wanna crawl under the rug.
I feel I've grown by leaps and bounds
Yet you still drive me into the ground.
So think ahead and don't make my blood boil
For I'm no crumbling like aluminum foil.

Age 47
Sept. 2003

A CAT NAMED TED

I hope he didn't die in pain
Eh, that cat in the lane.
He just lay there still
Yet he didn't have a medical bill.
Oh, that poor cat that lie dead
Maybe his name was Ted.

Age 47
Sept. 2003

TRUE LOVE

I love you very dearly
I cannot tell a simple lie;
I sure hope you don't move
'cause I'll NEVER say 'GOOD-BYE'.

I miss you even though
We're only two miles apart;
So please stay near
And don't ever depart.

I often think of you
Each awakening hour;
My thoughts of you remain
Always sweet and never sour.

You often said twice a week
Yet you readily bend the rules;
You accept and easily realize
When to use different tools.

You've a soft spot in your heart
This is oh—so true;
You pick me up and make me pink
After a day when I've been blue.

You are the meringue
In my Lemon Pie;
You are also the colorful rainbow
After a dreary, rainy sky.

I want you to know
You kept me from destruction;
You sure know how to give
God's Loving Grace and Instruction.

You are a honest and true friend
This I'll always know;
For whenever I see you
My heart throbs and I'm all aglow.

Age 47
Sept. 2003

PAINTED SKY

The dusk sunset paints with a mighty stroke
With rustic, burnt orange casting a hue;
It shows "God's Grandeur"[1] is at work
Across the horizon, the majestic view.

Then in the sky above waiting—expecting
Midnight violet, blue hovers;
It hangs and casts a mighty, nocturnal spell
As like an umbrella, it covers.

Around six along comes dawn
With it—the morning dew;
It brings forth a new day
And hopefully a beautiful sky of blue.

At noon, the sky is at its peak
And all is truly aglow;
The rays are beating down upon us
All this is the work of God—'I Know'.

1 Gerard Manley Hopkins

Age 47
Sept. 2003

HURRICANE ISABEL

Since I write poetry
lot of people asked me—
To write a poem about Isabel
And how the waves will swell.
Isabel is heading northwest
Putting many coastal people to the test.
Supplies and water are in demand
As Isabel prepares to strike land.
Plywood especially is selling like crazy
And no one appears to be lax or lazy.
It's bearing down on the mid coast
As schools and shelters are ready to host.
It's getting nearer to Carolina and Maryland
Where the trees are starting to bend.
Everyone is praying to keep power
So our food won't spoil and sour.
Some have decided to pack and flee
Rather than be battered by the rough sea.
I don't know about the plans for school
But an early closing for kids would be cool.
Yet parents have better things on their mind
As Isabel roars and comes from behind.
The trees are blowing, the clouds are thick
I just 'Thank God' my house is made of brick.
So it's time to batten down the hatches
And don't forget to lock the latches.
We even witnessed the calm before the storm
Which just so happens to be the norm.

The president is even thinking sound
He moved up to higher ground.
Yet the Yanks are playing in Baltimore
And wouldn't you know, it started to pour.
For the eye of the storm is getting near
Pretty soon it will be here.
Forecasters even said tornadoes may strike
As we all tell Isabel to take a hike.
Some areas will have great destruction
As our students receive science instruction.
Isabel has claimed a surfer's death
As most people hold their breath.
In fact after hearing the update
She's claimed more then twenty-eight.
All tolled there is a lot of damage
For some people, too much to manage.
In the aftermath, branches are strewn all around
As ocean communities try to rebound.

Age 47
Sept. 2003

MY MOTHER

Can't you just detect
That she is so very perfect;
So before you speak, reflect
On the words you'll select.

This is about no other
For it explains my mother;
Who is not like another
Alone, no sister or brother.

So here I must inject
That I'll pray and genuflect;
For a cause or effect
That she doesn't have a defect.

She watches every clothes' style
And cleans each kitchen tile;
Then her nails, she'll file
Summing up, reading awhile.

Age 47
Sept. 2003

ALCOHOL—HER SOURCE

Alcohol is her insulin
It's her sugar in disguise;
Whether it be vodka, whiskey or gin
It's leading to her demise.

It isn't fun living with a drunk
One who no longer eats;
She lies in bed as if in a fink
All huddled and curled in the sheets.

She yells and screams for no particular reason
It doesn't matter the day or time;
It doesn't even matter which season
For she even drinks at the flip of a dime.

Her whole character is markedly changed
After imbibing even more;
There are times she seems totally deranged
Especially when lying on the floor.

Some people say it's a pity
But I no longer feel remorse;
She even did this in Atlantic City
For as I said alcohol is her source.

Age 47
Sept. 2003

THE ONCOMING WINTER

As I woke up with a chill
I found my health going all downhill.
The night air is really brisk
That going out, in itself is a risk.
The weather is turning colder at best
As I try to fall asleep and rest.
Yet at times my bones feel frozen
Tempting me to visit Dr. Pilar or Rozen.
Yet the night air chill won't go away
In fact, for a while, it's here to stay.
Unfortunately ol man winter is about to come
As my poor body begins to turn numb.
It's horrendous to awake at four
Because I really want to sleep some more.
So I realize I have to pull the blankets higher
For my house has no place to light a fire.
Coming to my senses, I have to grin and bear it.
And just simply realize I'm not fit.
I close my eyes with bended knee
For extra sleep, to God I plea.

Age 47
October 2003

MOTHER TERESA (PART 2)

Mother Teresa left home at a tender eighteen
never once living the life of a queen
as she always appeared happy and serene.

After leaving she never saw her mother
nor her sisters or her brother
nevermore by a relative or another.

Yet for a time she felt abandoned
when I found out I was stunned
but she always gave donations to a "Fund".

Jesus asked her for a favor
to go out and be braver
So she asked Pope Pius XII for a waiver.

Mother Teresa was just that type
causing the press and media a lot of hype
as she took on the sari with a blue stripe.

She was meant to go forth amongst the poor
to pick up the ill from the floor
this was her mission to give them a lasting kiss for sure.

Mother Teresa really led an austere life
that to many would bring strife
only one bowl, spoon, fork and knife.

She did a lot more with less
and she really did confess
she despised being photoed by the press.

Each picture meant a soul in heaven
so snap, snap, snap—maybe seven
to Mother Teresa, hopefully eleven.

Quite a woman she was
never claiming anything as hers
that her whereabouts created a buzz.

She was a three decade superstar
even though she didn't own a car
but her feet would take her very far.

She flew a gratis—for free
as daily she prayed the Rosary
for simplicity was her Key.

Years ago, she cared for an orphan
who now is a Swiss Guard overseeing the Papal Van
and ready to greet many a fan.

So on the 19th the Pope made Blessed
and it was quite a fest
as we arose early and didn't get much rest.

It was truly worth the wait
as we were scanned, passing the gate
hoping not to arrive too late.

For yes, Mother Teresa was one of a kind
who never wined and dined
for she had the poor on her mind.

Age 47
Oct. 2003

THE 2003 WORLD SERIES

Up and down the Yankees went
This year far removed is Bucky Dent.
They started out winning
With players' faces grinning.
Then it was all tied at 1 apiece
And fans of both wouldn't cease.

All of a sudden, the Yanks were down 3-2
This World Series has taken a different view.
We are headed into game six
While bookies are placing their picks.
It'll be a disaster if they lose
For the Yankees ego will have a bruise.

Steinbrenner will blow his top
If the Yankees fall and flop.
Many heads will turn and spin
If indeed, they fail to win.
But tonite Petitte's on the mound
Throwing strikes on solid ground.

Yet our ace pitcher didn't have his stuff
So I guess the Boss will start to puff.
This year we indeed did lose to the "other team"
And within time the Boss will show his steam.

Age 47
Oct 2003

A FRIEND IN NEED

Just as if I heard a puppy's yelp
So too, our friend desperately needed help.
She wanted this, she wanted that
Yet confused, didn't know where she was at.
This is one time I stood up and roared
For this problem could not be ignored.
I actually pitied the driver and the poor soul
And her actions were starting to take a toll.
We were both on the edge of a brink
So I decided to play the "Shrink".
I never really had been in charge before
Until today when we were at the hospital's door.
I even had to call the clinician on staff
Making me want to cry instead of laugh.
I never, ever want to have this role again
For after today, I'm at my wits' end.

Age 47
Nov. 2003

MY ITALIAN TRIP

I started out down and miserable
The flight was bumpy and terrible
And the Alitalia staff rude and horrible.

The first hotel wasn't much better
I think Far & Wide will get a letter
Because I'm aggressive and a go-getter.

It didn't have a porter
And it wasn't worth a quarter
For G and A's spoiled, rotten daughter.

The first night didn't see much sleep
As I lay in bed curled up in a heap
Yet like Canada, many memories I'll keep.

On Wednesday we saw the Pope
With all his suffering, showed us hope
And taught us a lesson on how to cope.

I thought the Pontiff looked quite frail
As I pondered in my hotel, a converted jail
Yet I managed to buy relics on sale.

During the morn, the sun was out
As we all started to scream and shout
When J. P. took His Papal route.

But the azure sky soon turned a dismay gray
As we continued to pray
That the Pope will follow God's Way.

We celebrated Mass in Assisi
Where I got a Papal magazine for free
En route, we prayed the Rosary.

The magazine is simply beautiful
With yearly photos so ample
It was anything BUT dull.

The trip took hours and was long
I felt weak, instead of strong
At times I felt I didn't belong.

I endured and suffered through opera
Instead of "Good Morning" it was "Buona Sera"
I felt like I was going through a war.

First I agonized with Pavarotti
Then it was Andrea Bocelli
Neither of these really suit me.

While in Assisi we dined up the mountain
But the driver went too far and rolled back again
As we all prayed and counted to ten.

There are fast food places called Autogrill
Where you can really get your fill
If that is your earnest will.

*Each and every day brings **Pasta**.*
*Enough already—**Basta, Basta!***
After awhile it was no longer a fiesta.

Here the elevator is known as a lift
Going up and down—get my drift
So to me, this trip is my gift.

I must mention Marc for good measure
He's our tour guide and gives details with pleasure
I guess for our trip, he's our hidden treasure.

By this time I felt like an Italian resident
But in trying to speak, I lack their accent
Our third stop was Hotel President.

My housekeeper, Marisa, was a jewel
Which is not necessarily the rule
For some are fiery and have a lot of fuel.

I decided to use Friday for reflection
I thought about Mother Teresa's great mission
And her lack of want for television.

Saturday led us back to Rome
Our fourth and final home
And terrain of St. Peter's Dome.

The big celebration is yet to come
Which will make some of us numb
With Swiss Guard standing all aplomb.

This experience is for a select few
Who led life with a different view
Really knowing what to do.

Mother Teresa was just that type
Causing the media and press a lot of hype
As she took on the sari with a blue stripe.

With gates ajar, pandemonium broke out
As people from all over ran about
Putting seating arrangements in doubt.

Flags were waving here and there
In the brisk, cool autumn air
As the Pope took His Papal Chair.

The Pope said a beautiful Mass
It had a lot of pomp and class
And yes, each of us need a pass.

The ceremony lasted two hours
And Thank God there weren't any showers
But there were a lot of pretty flowers.

Afterwards I sadly departed
I was happy yet brokenhearted
For my poetry flew by, that which I started.

I was then able to change money
On this day which was very sunny
As Marc continued to be funny.

We returned and I ate in a deli-bar
Which was real close not very far
As my thoughts were on our new superstar.

The rest of the day was free
As I spent my time in the lobby
And watching the news on TV.

Monday brought us another Papal audience
Where he spoke and shared Mother's influence
And her lack of partiality or indifference.

Unfortunately it was hazy
Then it began to rain like crazy
As the day wore on, I grew lazy.

But after dinner, I got my desire
Which set my heart on fire
For I read my poem via French wire.

They told me to read with feeling
Even though there was noise from the ceiling
For this release gave me a healing.

I was overjoyed to spread His Word
Which finally will be heard
And certainly won't be ignored.

Tuesday brings more running around
As our trip is finally winding down
And soon we'll be homeward bound.

We saw St. Paul's
Behind the Roman Walls
And a lot of Coliseum halls.

Later on came the catacombs
Where Christian martyrs had their homes
As I continued my poems.

Tuesday night gave way to our final dinner
And with spaghetti I won't get thinner
And all this opera isn't making me a winner.

Age 47
Nov. 2003

ALL FED UP

President Bush, we're all fed up
Can't you see the blood filleth the cup?

Killing here, there and everywhere
And the Iraqis don't seem to care.

The killings are more and more
For this is a problem you can't ignore.

Please bring our troops home
So that their families won't spend time alone.

Age 47
Nov 2003

THE LUNAR ECLIPSE

The lunar eclipse was a majestic sight
On a clear, spectacular, autumn, Saturday Night.
Its apex occurred around eight
On this November 9th, the fixed date.
The moon turned a dark rustic hue
It gave spectators a wondrous, beautiful view.
I sat out, bundled on my front porch
As this magnificent, rare event came forth.
For the Earth and Sun are aligned with the Moon
The next one is in October which can't come too soon.

Age 47
November 2003

I'm a Human Too

I'm a Human too
I may make mistakes
I get into debates;
Sometimes I fight
'Cause I want to be right.
But I'm a human too.

I'm a human too
I need friends, not foes
In this land of woes;
I want to be brave
For the love I crave.
Yet I'm a human too.

I'm a human too
I only look after me
And can be a stringing bee;
At times I don't care
Yet I know it's not fair.
For I'm a human too.

I'm a human too
I may whine and cry
Then tell the world "Good-Bye";
At times I'll shout
And even begin to pout.
Yet I'm a human too.

Yes. I'm a human too.
I have varied views
And also get the blues;
For life is an uphill battle
With people acting like cattle.
Still I'm a human too.

Age 47
Dec. 2003

The Birthmark

Lets make one thing clear
Just don't stare, don't sneer;
For on my face I have a birthmark
So I can't be compared to a Lark.
It's just not right to give grief
So let me give advice that's brief;
Please don't look, please don't stare
For it's not right, Christian or fair.
Our Lord made us all diff'rent
And this mark is what I was sent;
It sets me apart from the rest of you.
So don't sit there are stew.
When you see my birthmark don't sneer
For to my eye you'll bring a tear.

Age 47
Dec. 2003

Gerry

Gerry—you are my back drop
You are the cream of the crop.
When I encountered you
It was like a sweet honeydew.
You are like our sweet Maxine
And the spring grass turning green.
You are the zip in my lemon pie
You are the shimmering star in the sky.
You mean so very much to me
And I hope I do equally.

Age 47
Dec. 2003

What is Christmas?

What is Christmas?—Let me tell you
It is meant for one to pray in the pew.

The "C" is for the newborn babe, "Christ Jesus."
The "H" is for this "Holy Day."
The "R" is for "Rabbonah."
The "I" is for "Immanuel" they say.
The "S" is for the "Shining Star."
The "T" is for "Teacher."
The "M" is for "Mary", his mother."
The "A" is for "Artistic Preacher."
The final "S" is for the "Son of God."

For us, Jesus Christ, Teacher,
Rabbi and Preacher, get a firm nod.

Age 47
Dec. 2003

The Grinch

Instead of wounds healing
People are out stealing.
Instead of singing to the ceiling
There is a lack of Christ's feeling
Even though Church bells are pealing.

For now I'd rather be in a bubble
As for me, God didn't make a double.
At times I feel like trashy rubble
Just like an old man's bearded stubble.

You see, it's Christmas—time of the Grinch
It's a time when I flinch.
For I'm not as pretty as a finch
I have to make do in a pinch
And this season is no cinch.

At times I'd rather crumble
Because God didn't make me humble.
I have flaws and so I fumble
When angry under my breath I mumble.

So yes—the Grinch is back
Giving everyone a lot of flack.
He could be Mick or even Mack
Or perhaps even Mr. Jack
Yet the Grinch will always give you a slack.

Age 47
Dec. 2003

Ugh, Another Christmas

"Bah—humbug" Scrooge Says
I wish I were in Port Fez.

The gifts are trickling in
While my patience wears thin.
I cannot go to Spain.
Because I never booked a plane.

"Bah—humbug" Scrooge Implores
For this season I deplore.

Cards are being mailed out
While I sit, cry and pout.
I can't go to my aunt
'Cause she can't pant.

"Bah—humbug" Scrooge Screams
I wish I had other dreams.

Tis the time of the year
That I truly, truly fear.
Now the Great Depresssion starts
Knowing gifts are from empty hearts.

"Bah—humbug" Scrooge Rages
I feel like I'm in a cage.

This holiday is so phony
And so full of baloney.
All I get is a lot of stress
And so for now I could care less.

"Bah—humbug" Scrooge Yells
In stark contrast to Silver Bells.

Therefore I look to flee
And elsewhere find some glee.
And so remain the sane
I think of lovely Spain.

Age 47
Doreen 2003

Christmas

"C" Tis the Season to be Calm

"H" Tis the Season to stop the Harm.

"R" Tis the Season for the Reason

"I" Tis the Season for the Isaian.

"S" Tis the Season to make a faith Statement

"T" Tis the season to read the New Testament.

"M" Tis the season not to Mourn

"A" Tis the season to Adorn

"S' Tis the season the Eternal Son is born.

Age 47
Dec. 2003

End of 2003

It's the end of the year
Time to start 2004 with cheer.
Let this new year 'O four
Bring with it peace and the end of war.
Let us start to act humane
For the otherwise life is insane.
Let us end the hardship and hate
Let each man find a suitable mate.
Let's start the year with a bit more joy
Give a young child a game or toy.
Lets not act with stupidity or haste
But rather have good manners and taste.
Make someone's day by saying "Hello"
Or just treat someone to a little jello.
Let "V" stand for "Victory"
Let this be a new page inventory in History.
But please let it not stand for "victims"
For there have been too many funerals and hymns.

Age 47
Dec 2003

Extraterrestrial

We went to the moon
But it wasn't in June.
We landed in July
Amidst the warm summer sky.
In '04 we're headed for Mars
Millions of miles from the stars.
We're searching for the extraterrestrial
By researching our ancestral.
So by learning our past isn't bad
And with our accomplishments we can't be sad.

Age 47
Jan 2004

Michael Jackson

Michael Jackson is a piece of work
He's very dif'rent from yesteryear
He grew up popular with the Jackson Five
But his weirdness makes most jeer.

He's held his baby out a window—
He's slept in bed with young boys
He's done some real crazy things
Instead of using his money for toys.

He's being brought up on charges
He's meeting up with nasty fate.
After court, he danced on his car
And late night hosts will use him as bait.

After the trial, he returned to the Neverland Ranch
For his fans he threw a big feast
Judge said "Off on the wrong foot"
But Jackson couldn't care in the least.

It's a shame it's come to this
He was once so popular
Pretty soon, gone are his rights
His house, land and maybe his car.

Age 47
Jan. 2004

The Meaning of Love

Love doesn't show sorrow
Nor does it want for t'morrow
And love you need not borrow.

Love is meant to be gentle
Thus obtaining a suite rental
And no longer being parental.

Love is meant for two
In all that you say and do
And have the same point of view.

Love is patient and kind
It helps when one is blind
Or when the partner has a troubled mind.

Love is sweet and tender
It treats your ego as a fender bender
And doesn't look at your gender.

Love comes from God
Who made you form earthen sod
And thus bestows his nod.

Age 47
Jan. 2004

Celebrating Fifty

Celebrating fifty
Can be oh, so nifty.

Especially when you're young at heart
And stay together not apart.

Oh, at times you indeed did fight
But most of the time you saw the light.

The joy, the pain, the sorrow
Yet all for a better tormorrow.

Life together can be a dream
Because both of you make a great team.

So fifty is a long time you see
And I pray continued happiness for thee.

Age 47
Jan. 2004

Fifty Years

You've made it through fifty long years
Amidst joy and sorrow, love and some tears.
Life's had its tweaks of ups and downs
And even circles on the merry-go-round.
Some times have probably been dubious
While other occasions have been glorious.
I'm sure the latter outweighs the former
In doing so you had to be the conformer.
Marriage has had its struggles you see
Yet I bet more happy days helped make it to fifty.
So we all gather here today
To start you an another fifty without delay.
Happy Anniversary to a fine pair
May God Bless and Take Care.

Age 47
Jan 2004

Golden Anniversary

Fifty years ago you were a groom
And you a beautiful wife.
You both went to the altar
And in thee, you did confide.

Youth made you lovers
Holy Matrimony made you one.
Nothing can stop or put asunder
What God hath begun.

Before the altar and many witnesses
A priest made you man and wife.
For better or for worse
For happy times and in strife.

So celebrating your honored fifty
While you're still young at heart.
Can be quite nifty
Just stay together and don't part.

With the joy, pain and sorrow
It's a long time you see.
I hope you have a better tomorrow
And continue to live happily.

Age 47
Jan. 2004

Capt. Kangaroo

On this January 24th, Capt. Kangaroo died today
Yet he and his memories are here to stay.

He died at a young Seventy-six
Giving lots of children their kicks.

At first he played Clarabel, the Clown
And never gave anyone a frown.

He played Tinker, the Toymaker
But he was never in a kitchen as a baker.

Bob Keeshan's main gig was Capt. Kangaroo
Where he had all the animals and a comical zoo.

As the Captain he had a bowl haircut
And he was never down or in a rut.

In fact he always chose to smile
Putting a grin on the fame of many a child.

He enjoyed children so very much
And the Captain had a unique touch.

So certain ads he would fetch
Such as Play Doh & Etch a Sketch.

He'd stroll through his Treasure House
With Mr. Frog & Mr. Moose but never a mouse.

His sidekick was Mr. Green Jeans
Who often told you to eat veggies and beans.

Knock-Knock jokes were told by Mr. Moose
For he was lively and very loose.

So was the character, Dancing Bear
And Grandfather Clock at which he did stare.

Another character was Banana Man
Who had mass appeal and many a fan.

All in all his lessons were basic
And he'll be remembered as a classic.

Age 47
Jan. 2004

Fame

Something's in the air
In fact, its' all about.
You're moving up and up
And its' a thing called clout.

You write a book
And get some notoriety.
It all started out
With a bit of poetry.

You are suddenly wanted
The phone rings and rings.
You feel like one
Of the Three-Kings!

Where I'm headed
I do not know.
Offers come in
But I pray they don't go.

Age 47
Jan. 2004

Love and Marriage

How did dad find her?
It was at an Italian dance.
Certainly not wearing a fur
Yet her slim body did enhance.

Where did they meet?
It was downtown New York.
He swept her off her feet
After awhile, popped the cork.

When did she join him?
It was 50 years today.
Both were full of vigor and vim
Both then and now May 2nd.

What drew them to each other?
It was a personal magnetism.
Soon they were one together
Fused like the edge of a prism.

Why did their marriage hold?
*The answer is basic—**Pure Love***
This type is so solid is hard to fold
For it was a match made from above.

Age 47
May, 2, 2004

A New Decade

Get it done
In "O One"

Please be true
In "O two"

Come and See
In "O Three"

Score some more
In "O Four"

Come Alive
In "O Five"

Get your kicks
In "O Six"

You're near Heaven
In "O Seven"

First the Pearly Gates
In "O eight"

Please be mine
In "O Nine"

Age 47
Feb. 2004

Terror

Twisted, mangled bodies
Spewing forth blood.

Terror . . . Terror

Fear, Pain, Anguish
Lives lost needlessly
Where do we go now?
What do we do now?

Terror . . . Terror

It grips the sincere
It puts a stranglehold
On the innocent victims.
Seizes them in their Path.

Terror . . . Terror

Mangled trains askew
Like twisted pretzels.
Yet God reigns.
Peace will prevail
In Spain.

Age 47
March 11, 2004

Atocha

Agonia

Terror

Odio

Catastrofe

Horror

Amor Siempre

Age 47
March 2004

Espana

Esperanza

Sinceridad

Paz

Amistad

Neque

Alegria

Age 47
March 2004

Life of the Cat

She leaps onto my bed
She's got big bold
Wide green eyes.
They're staring directly at you.
She looks inquisitively
Very intently
Mews/meows then
Saunters off the quilt.
Mom and Dad are fast asleep
No longer on her lap—Now
She depends on me, the
Other sole partner.
Loving company
Maxine accompanies
Dad, then Mom
And for nocturnal bliss
Finds a happy home
On the den quilt.

Contented, we are all asleep
Until the moon sets and the
Sun rises for the
Next day chores.
Then she is up
And about' running,
Dashing down the hall
Looking to play.
Then she settles down by
Bird watching in the window.
She'll catnap and catch
A snooze here or there.

When Dad comes home however
She's all his. She
Bounds onto the desk with
Such agility, She lays near
His letter opener. Sometimes
On his paperwork. After being
Stroked she begins to purr. She is
Now content.

Her master is home at last.

Age 47
March 2004

Sister Luke

She's a Sister of Charity
Yet her name isn't Beth.
Instead she is Sister Luke
And she's as calm as a duke.
She hales from Kentucky
And seems to be carefree.
Yet she lives in Ohio
And is always on the go.
Sister travels back and forth
From the deep south to the north.
She has a seven hour commute
Instead of a habit, she wears a suit!

Age 47
April 2004

The Retreat Weekend

I spent the weekend on retreat
When I went to Nazareth, Kentucky
The nuns were thoughtful and warm
And the girls were so jolly.
We prayed and shared
Our hearts were set free
Everything was simply terrific
And everyone was oh, so friendly.

They were all so kind and understanding
Nazareth showed such hospitality
In the sharing, the Sisters were open minded
As they shared their generosity.
Deep down they were simply fabulous
As they showed their congeniality
They were patient and tolerant
And we ended with gaity.

Age 47
April 2004

Creation

God made the heavens and the earth
And He made everything of worth.
The void was named the sky
Which was miles up high.
'Twas the end of the first day
Yet God did not play.
God separated the sea from the land
And put all vegetation into the sand.
The second day passed
Yet God did not fast.
God created vegetation, trees and fruit
And many things that have a root.
Eve and morn came and passed: day three
God saw it was good and showed glee.
He made the Sun to shine by day
And the Moon to reign when light turns grey.
Thus was day four
But God would create more.
He created many types of fish
And separated them from the bird and fowl dish.
After the fifth day, God didn't rest
For He was to create His best.
Then Male and Female, He created each
To rule over birds, animals, fish and beach.
This was on day six
When he completed his eartlly mix.

He rested on the seventh day
And set it aside to rest and pray.

Age 48
April 20005

Our Parish Spring Dance

St. John's held a spring dance
And "Hawaii night" was the theme
As couples took their stance
I began to smile and beam.

The night was peaceful yet full of fun
Parrots decorated the walls
Everyone was there, even a nun
And garlands draped the halls.

We all had good balance
As Gerry and I made a great team
Oldies music did enhance
As the night roared on with full steam.

We ended by dancing just as we had begun
And no-one took a serious fall
When the night was almost done
We had the fifty-fifty call.

Age 47
April 2004

Two Different Worlds

My cat is sleeping
On my heart—
My heart that's weeping
Weeping for those killed
Killed in the war.
My heart is filled
With feelings of anger and rage
With fear—
My thought is still.
While we turn another page—
Another page of history
Or shall I say Her Story
That of Jessica Lynch
Free as a spring time finch.

Age 47
May 2004

Don Quixote

Don Quixote, dreamer of an impossible dream
Don Quixote and Sancho Panza-a great team.

Coming form an area La Mancha near Seville
Although a prison was not all that evil.

Don Quixote with a dream to fulfill
To go off and fight a giant—eh a windmill.

He fought by using his sword and imagination
He would later face severe interrogation.

He never got any real, sufficient rest
Reaching for impossible quest.

Reaching for Aldonza-Dulcenea
Was his real, surreal, idea.

Age 47
May 2004

A Warm Night

Warm spring night
Lit up with fright,
Lightening has appeared
As we walk with our endeared.

Torrential rain cometh down
Throughout my small town,
The FM radio now has static
Yet thunder is above my attic.

I hope it will soon stop
For into my bed I flop.

Age 47
May 2004

My Day at Bally's

I went to gamble at Bally's
Wow the money surely tallies.
Initially I spent all but twenty
But later on I counted plenty.
I sat in the casino with rugs so plush
As I started to hit flush after flush.
At times I got a full house
As I sat quiet as a mouse.
Once or twice I got four of a kind
Which got me out of my economic bind.
All in all, I had a wonderful time
As I won quarters and nickels, but never a dime.
I spent some on a fluffy toy
It looks more like a girl than a boy.
The dog is purple and pink
And has a necklace with a link.
I also bought a cheap blue visor.
With summer coming it could not be wiser.

Age 47
May 2004

Searching

I often ask
What is my task?
Where is my place
In this rat race?
I come and go
Passing friend and foe.
Will I find my way
As I pass though each day?

Age 47
May 2004

Friendship

I found a new friend
Will she stay till the end?
Her name is Mary.
Will she help me?
I'm short, she is tall.
Will our friendship
Flourish or stall?
She is willing to collaborate
At some future date.

Age 47
May 2004

On Hold

Perhaps Barnes and Noble in July
As Mary has an answer to my "Why?"
She said she'd like to read with me
But that will be after school, you see.
Teaching Spanish has been a dream
As I'm about to go ahead with full steam.
So yes, my book is on hold
As I try to finish my mold.

Age 47
May 2004

Thoughts of Gerry

I was crying
In the midst of flying.
Just thinking of him
Hoping days won't be dim.

I called, he didn't respond
I called, for broken is our bond.
Well, at least temporarily
While I'm at school, you see.

Although I desire to learn
As a human, it's Gerry I yearn.
Being alone is no fun
Even though I'm with a lovely nun.

Age 48
May 29 2004

Sister Mary Madden

Sister gives me encouragement and hope
Though I don't like her "Ivory" soap.
She's very understanding and compassionate
As she spread out her "Welcome Mat."
After we kissed, settled and said "Hello"
Sister let me make lime "Jello."
A few days to go before my class
I sure hope I do well and pass.
I'm into ESL, she was into History
A difference that makes her, her and me, me.
But we are under the same sign
Which to me is fine.
We are those unpredictable twins
Only difference, Sister has less sins!

Age 48
May 2004

Memorial Day

Just what is Memorial Day?
It really isn't a day to be happy or gay.
This is a day for thought and sorrow.
And to pray for a better tomorrow.
It's a day to remember those who've gone
ahead.
It's time to remember our forgotten dead.
It certainly shouldn't be a day for mall
hopping.
Or for grocery, food or clothes shopping.
We should remember heroes of the past.
And stop all these crazy wars at last.

Age 48
May 2004

He Fell In Love

He fell in love with me
That was a summer cicada, you see.
He nestled in my big toe
He stayed and didn't want to go.
At times they can be very noisy
And they're striped like a huge bee.
To Washingtonians, he's a foe
And a cause of a lot of woe.
Yet this cicada tickled me
Waiting for a bus under an oak tree.

Age 48
June 2004

My Teacher, Vance

My teacher's name is Vance
I wonder if he can dance.
He asked me to write a poem
I'll write of LADO, not home.
At times classes are hard you see.
So I ought to study and not get a D.
I'm learning to teach others ESL
Getting a job will be just swell!
Every afternoon we have a practicum
Gosh—I sure hope that I don't appear dumb.
After a week, school was punctured by Death
It gave not only me, but the nation a breath.
President Reagan passed away
His funeral was on my 48th birthday.
Oh gosh, oh golly, oh gee
After this I wonder what will become of me?

Age 48
June 2004

President Reagan's Death

President Reagan died the other day
Turning Washington streets into a maze.
Some of the normal folk are mad
And it's driving me to an insane craze.

I can't imagine a "shut-down Washington"
Streets will close, traffic will abound.
People will stand twenty deep
As helicopters fly high over the ground.

Foreign journalists will be covering it
News shots and aerials will take place.
People from all walks pay respects
And dignitaries will flow at a steady pace.

Today is Wednesday, the ninth of June
The body was flown in late.
He was taken from the airport
To the Capital to lie in state.

Everyone paying their respects
Black, white, young and old.
After Reagan took office,
Communism sort of went cold.

President Bush flew back to town
For on Friday, Reagan will be eulogized.
The President is preparing his remarks
As last minute's plans are finalized.

It's late night and there are still throngs
Since the funeral is for a selected few.
The route will take hold
On Massachusetts and Wisconsin Avenue.

Age 48
June 2004

Delving into LADO

I'm so glad to be at LADO in D.C.
I'm having so much fun, can't you see?

We teach about language and also of sports
We help each other with our reports.

It's fun to learn in a different setting
I just wish my cat were here for petting.

I miss her and she misses me
That's our one problem of being in D.C.

But I'm enjoying school a whole lot
Even though the weather is quite hot.

June down here in D.C. is just like New York
As I start my next lesson with a bowl and fork.

We're giving orderly directions for gazpacho
I wonder if I should have brought a nacho.

Age 48
June 2004

The Great Communicator Silenced

June 11th will go down in history.
Oh, no, hot because of my birthday.
It's now a national day of mourning, you see.
President Reagan will return to his earthen clay.

The heavens over Washington opened wide.
The rain was noted as the nation cried.
Feelings that most people can't hide.
For this was the day of national mourning.

Lady Thatcher was there is spirit.
Heads of State abound from every nation.
I understand Ronnie was full of wit.
His wisdom is passing through our generation.

The eulogies offered are splendid.
A lot of stories are being told.
History is being recorded.
Of a man who was so brave and bold.

By trying to plant democratic seeds
He was known as a "Liberator."
He had a charm tailored to others' needs
Hence, Reagan was known as the Great
Communicator.

Age 48
June 2004

Mother Teresa—A Pen

Mother Teresa was a pen in God's hand
Just doing each of His commands.
She said she was just an instrument
That which Our Lord God hath sent.
She loved all types of human life
And saw Jesus even in the midst of strife.
In a typical sari that she wore
Mother Teresa reached out to the poor.
Her prayer life was twenty four-seven
Knowing this is the path to heaven.
One young girl wanted to join her
Mother asked her to return to her father.
Mother Teresa knew the girls' place was at home
Under her mother and father's dome.

Age 48
June 2004

Washingtonians

Washingtonians are great people
AS I bid farewell near a church's steeple.
Everyone here is nice and they live a slower pace
Contrary to New York and New Jersey's rat race.
At times I really felt like I was in Spain
I even got to take their meticulous train.
Everything here is spic and span, neat and clean
And they are helpful, far from being mean.
Even the weather here is superb
As I ponder the powerful tenses of the verb.
Well Good-bye Washington as I head back
Good-bye to my teachers, and Andy, and Rissa and
Mack.

Age 48
June 26, 2004

E S L

I have a lot of remorse
Now that I've finished my ESL course.
To continue with another source.

Studying is wonderful indeed
For it plants knowledge as a seed.
A true, basic instinctive need
Yet not knowing where it may lead.

My life is clearer than before.
Where once I stumbled upon a shut door.
Now with ESL training, there are jobs galore
Hoping one will be in Spanish folklore.

Madrid, Granada, Sevilla or Toledo
I'll go without any "Miedo".
Teaching both Alfred and Alfredo
Having God as the main Credo.

Age 48
June 2004

Autumn

As autumn leaves
Begin to tumble,
Football players
Start to fumble.

Slippery and wet roads
Will make me stumble,
And then bad words
My mouth will mumble.

Then with clenched fist
A paper I'll crumble,
As this Christian
Could be more humble.

Age 48
Oct 2004

The Coming of Fall

The leaves are turning amber
As Martha Stewart stews in the slammer.
The sun is setting on another day
As we find out Gov. McGreevy is gay.
Fall seems to be here at last
With the Yanks losing, all are aghast.
The pouring rain is at its worse
While the Bosox try to rid their curse.
Rain, tornadoes, and hurricanes galore
All amidst crazy, political folklore.
October days are drawing to an end
Yet Bush and Kerry don't seem to bend.
The mighty winds are brisk and stiff
As politicians are on the edge of a cliff.
November is quickly approaching
As Senator Kerry is reproaching.
Each day and night seems to be colder
As we learn of the death of still another soldier.

Age 48
Oct. 2004

My New Friend

My new friend's name is Mary
She calls me sweetie and at times honey;
I think she'll even take care of me
Even if my nose is runny.

We both have a lot in common
Both of us write poetry;
We like animals; especially cats
So we have a lot of symmetry.

But we differ
Mary is 5'10'—very tall;
I am quite the opposite
Being 5'—so small.

When I was cold
She searched for a sweater.
Friends like Mary
Don't come much better.

Age 48
Nov. 2004

Poetry In Animals

If you see an asp—
Watch out or he'll grasp.
Seeing a black bear—
Can be quite rare.
Owning a domestic cat—
Is where I'm at.
Walking a friendly dog—
Is better than the morgue.
Seeing an Asian elephant—
Will make you rant.

Observing a sly fox—
Is better than eating lox.
Watching the zoo's gorilla—
Maybe his name is Magilla.
Learning to ride a horse—
Is when you'll need a course.
So, you want an iguana—
Afterwords take a sauna
Say you've seen a jackal—
Well I'll say "Holy Mackerel"!

Holding a baby koala—
Is like an Australian gala.
Owning a spotted leopard—
Is not good for a Shepherd.
After seeing a mouse—
You'll run into the house.
Ever see a nanny goat—
Try to swim or float?
Eating a fried octopus—
Followed by some couscous.

Riding a pony—
  Is nothing phony.
Catching a hundred quail—
  Is quite a long tale.
Pulling out a rabbit—
  Is a magician's habit.
Cooking a snake—
  Can't be as good as steak.
Bring a green toad—
  Into your abode.

In seeing a unicorn—
  You'll observe only one horn!
It's hideous to see a vulture—
  In any modern culture.
Looking at a whale—
  Will make you look frail.
Owing a yak—
  Is something I lack.
Lastly there's Zoey the zebra—
  Singing alone to "Abra Cadabra."

Age 48
July 2004

When?

When will there be peace?
When will all wars cease?
When will men get along?
When will we be able to sing a happy song?
When will we whistle and be carefree?
When will there be joy and harmony?
When will we see eye to eye?
When will we stop living a great big lie?
When will wealth be spread among men?
When will we have a gun and weapons ban?
When will we be clothed from head to foot?
When will good ideas take hold and stay put?
When will we heed Mother Teresa's advise?
When will we care for others and be nice?

When we put down guns and armor—That's when!
When we get along with our neighbors-
Then and "Only Then"!

Age 48
Dec. 2004

Who?

Who is your father, your mother?
Who is your sister, your brother?
Do they live near or afar?
Do they watch you like a shining star?

Who is your nearest and best friend?
Who is really there until the end?
Are they with you when you stray?
Are they really watching you day by day?

Who is the person living next door?
Is it really your friendly neighbor?
Does she drop in or care for thee?
Maybe none does, but Jesus does you see!

Age 48
Dec 2004

For Jesus

Jesus, Just for Us

E en route to/ from Emmaus

Sanctus Spiritus

Umbrella of the Universe

Savior to All of US

Age 48
Dec. 2004

God's Presence at Mass

Oh God-come into my soul
Oh God-won't you make me whole?
You come in the form of Bread and Wine
This our Eternal Supper on which we need to dine.
The Bread/Wafer is Blest—then broken.
A sign of your splintered bones—a token.
God's Body is what You gave to us
You hung on the cross—didn't make a fuss.
The Wine is our Spiritual Drink
Whether red or white it is our link.
God's blood was shed for each
Hoping we'll soon be within your reach.
So God—even though I often sin
Won't you forget, enter and come in?

Age 48
Dec. 2004

A Cold

It's back to square one
Seems as this cold has just begun.
I had it really bad last week
And medical advice I did seek.
Coughing and sneezing and aching bones
Many calls to the doctor on the phones.
She said, "meds, fluids and bed rest"
Darn, I wish this cold would go out west.
Here we go with "Vick's Vaporub"
I'd rather be eating a tuna sub.

Age 48
Jan. 2005

In Memoriam of Mary Ann

"This too Shall Pass"
As Mary Ann left behind class.
Mary Ann was a St. Elizabeth grad
With a home economics degree that she had.
She grew up with style and grace
As she always had a smiling face.
She was a teacher of highest quality
With a high sense of ethics and morality.
It may take some time to heal
For emotions are truly real.
I'm sure you'll do just fine
Just place your trust in Thine.

Age 48
Jan. 2005

Out West

Sitting by the side of a train
People watch the ghastly, pouring rain.
Earthquakes, torrents and mudslides prevail
As we hear the anguished people wail.
They are losing their homes every day
As news reports that another is washed away.
Lives and families have been destroyed
And lots of folks are now unemployed.
The children can't learn, can't even play
They just sit around dismal day by day.
At first, I thought the tsunami was bad
But California and Nevada are just as sad.
Money and funds are being routed all around
As 3 more bodies have been found.
The Midwest has an avalanche of snow
It seems that this '05, the weather is our foe.
On one road there was a 25 car pile-up
But on the bright side, I saw a rescue of a pup.

Age 48
Jan. 2005

An Unwelcomed Pimple

Why is it that you came?
Don't you have any shame?
You come on my face
To many nations and every race.
You come on a nose, then a chin
You show up all over facial skin.
Some people call you acne, other zits.
Let's just say you look like shit.
You rule supreme and make a mess
You cause all teenagers a lot of stress.
You're full of goo and pus
Is it any wonder kids make a fuss?
So why don't you just go away?
For nobody wants you to stay.

Age 48
Jan. 2005

Portrait of a Priest

What really makes a good priest?
Is it his ability to celebrate the Lord's feast?
Is it hearing hours of confessions
And then granting fair absolutions?
Does he enjoy celebrating Communion
Showing that Our Lord was once Human?
Is it an internal love for nature and people?
Is it blessing himself in front of a steeple?
Is it giving a good sermon week after week
Or is it being able to listen rather than speak?
Is he able to perform a ceremonial marriage
With or without the horse and carriage?
Will he be there for the baby's Baptism?
Will he see God's truth like light through a prism?
Will he express sorrow during the Last Rites
Yet explaining that there are better heights?
He'll recite and pray the "Liturgy of the Hours"
And on the Altar, he'll place the flowers.
Does he look forward to Adoration
And especially Mary's Coronation?
Does he pray often to Our Lady . . . Mary
Especially by reciting the Rosary?
He celebrates Happiness, shares in grief and sorrow
Yet he always hopes for a better tomorrow.

Age 48
Jan. 2005

A Tsunami

The Asian earth quaked
And thousands are being waked.
Disaster struck eleven nations
As governments started evacuations.
Many have become refugees
As they fell down and begged on their knees.
Many children have been orphaned
While American hearts have been softened.
They no longer have fathers or mothers
They're being cared for by considerate others.
Some were saved by climbing a tree
Others by holding on to debris.
There are organizations like the Red Cross and CARE
Trying to raise funds and clothes for people to wear.
People are donating at every level
From a tsunami believed to be caused by the devil.
So far four billion has been raised
As many people are still dazed.
Emotional wounds will take years to heal
As most Christians pray and kneel.
Climatic happenings are hard to control
So better warning systems remain our goal.

Age 48
Jan. 2005

President Bush's Second Term

The inauguration was a blast
President Bush had his day at last.
His finished the oath with "So Help Me God"
As he gave his faith an affirmative nod.
He is starting his second term
Amidst many commitments that are firm.
One thing is a change to Social Security
Affordable housing is another priority.
After the inauguration, there was a parade
He walked part of the route and wasn't afraid.
Police stood about at 20 foot stations
And representatives flew in from many nations.
The hordes of people were festive all around
Creating a spirit of gaiety rarely found.
Then there was a respite, a time to eat
Where at the head table, he took his seat.
After the meal, 'twas time to hit the town
For they changed into black tie and gown.
He and the First Lady danced the night away.
Then went to bed, after a long, long day.

Age 48
Jan. 2005

Winter's Blast

Winter started early
Just three weeks into the year;
With heavy snow blowing
And people walking in fear.

The wind and breeze were stiff
Three states called an emergency;
People should behave and treat each other
In a state of human decency.

This was a true nor'easter
But simply put, it's a blizzard;
This weather isn't fit for man
In fact, not even for a poor lizard.

It is now eleven p.m.
Lots of crashes, conditions deteriorate;
More snow will be coming later
To keep warm just cuddle with your mate.

It steadily approached us
It came from the Midwest;
It hit Michigan, Wisconsin and Ohio
You can't even keep warm with a vest.

Age 48
Jan. 2005

A Great Bowling Night

Bowling tonight was so much fun
It was like basking in the sun.
I had a high game of one forty three
That's why I was so very happy.
I got a strike and then a spare
It was as good as enjoying an éclair.
At one point I had two strikes
At this point I wanted others to take a hike.
Scoring good was like a breeze
Yet it seems like a great big tease.
I really don't bowl this well
So all 'n all, this night was swell.

Age 48
Jan. 2005

After Bowling

After bowling really great
I spent the night watching TV;
I was glued to it
For a storm is coming you see.
The forecasters are predicting
Up to 2 inches per hour;
With this crazy weather
You certainly won't see a flower.
As a matter of fact
They're calling it a blizzard;
This crazy, awful weather
Isn't fit for a lizard.
People are stocking up
On groceries and milk;
And with these temperatures
No one is wearing silk.
The plows are in full gear
They are ready to go;
They will hit the roads
After the first major snow.

Age 48
Jan. 2005

Johnny Carson

Johnny Carson died on January 23rd
He was a true comedian;
He was on late night TV
After New York, he was a Californian.

Johnny began his career many years ago
He was the host of "Who Do you Trust?"
He was humble, without superego
Sympathies are pouring in from dawn to dusk.

He did the "Tonight Show" for 30 years
Johnny took over for Jack Paar;
He saw everyone as his peer
And he helped form many a star.

He was very humble and sincere
He was very down to earth;
With over 27,000 guests and no fear
He treated each with dignity and worth.

Johnny didn't like a lot of fanfare
He was a very private person;
He had a genius that was rare
These are the tings that made Johnny Carson.

Age 48
Jan. 2005

Karen Gutfhall

Karen Gutfhall is my social worker
But she's also a true friend;
She sees each and every task
Thru 'til the very end.

Her job consumes a lot of time
Sometimes she's on the road;
In her line of work
She has a certain ethics code.

Sometimes it's paperwork
Sometimes she'll make a call;
And then she'll meet me
Down in the Borough Hall.

She'll call this or that
She'll go the extra mile;
She does her job great
And greets you with a smile.

Age 48
Jan. 2005

Palisades Park

Palisades Park is such a mess,
This is sadly true, I must confess.
Papers and litter are strewn here and there,
Plastic bottles blocking sewers everywhere.
Snow is still covering some hydrants,
And this town doesn't have enough plants.
Years ago it was such a pretty town,
With people being nice and no-one having a frown.
Today, others come and toil,
And then throw the trash onto the soil.
On Broad Avenue stores are boarded up,
And old men stand and spit in a cup.
There used to be a song, "Down at Palisades Park."
There's no more A&P or 5 & 10 cent store,
Nothing is like it was before!

Age 48
Jan. 2005

My Cat, Maxine

I found my cat on my bed
Yet she was under the spread.
She appeared as a massive lump
Sort of like a big bump.
Then she laid on my lap
And decided to take her nap.
As I stroked her, she purred
For my cat is not a nerd.
Then she'll rub your legs
Especially for the food she begs.

Age 48
Jan. 2005

Dream, Dream, Dream

Dream, Dream, Dream
Children—That of Ice Cream.
Every night I dream
Of hallucinating screams.
Most men will dream
Of having a winning team.
Parents will continually dream
Of children with a facial beam.

So dream if you must
And don't let your dreams rust.

Dream well
I hope it's swell.
But don't dream of hell
Or of a jail cell.
Dream and don't tell
And your dreams will gel.
Dream of the Liberty Bell
Just dream on and don't yell.

So dream if you will
And dream 'til you have your fill.

Age 48
Feb. 2005

A Simpler Time

There was a time
When life was simple;
It was a long time ago
When I had a pimple.

Nothing boring, no chores
And certainly no stress;
Today with work and wars
Life is such a mess.

All hell breaks loose
In many a way;
And in my life
I hardly have any say.

Doing the laundry
Shopping in the stores;
Standing at bus lines
Such lousy, boring chores.

Age 48
Feb. 2005

Reunion Meeting

I really had such a great night,
And being with old classmates was a delight.
The only spoiler was the weather,
But camaraderie couldn't be better.
Kenny played host and opened his house,
And none of us sat quiet like a mouse.
We threw out ideas onto the floor,
Although it took some time to get to the core.
We spoke abut hotels and prices,
Now I'm wondering if the cost would be a crisis.
There was certainly no silence,
Yet it was a great experience.
We brought back yesteryear today,
As each of us had our say.
Sean and Catherine brought up antidotes,
After reading my letter, they then took notes.
There really is no need to boast,
For Kenny was the perfect host.
It was a shame to say "Good-Bye",
As the night sure did fly.

Age 48
Feb. 2005

An Aging Pontiff

Our "Holy Father" isn't well
And this news isn't swell.
He had a severe relapse of the flu
Which had made all his fans blue.
We want him to get much better
So we send our prayers in the form of a letter.
We all wish him a speedy return
For this is one thing we all yearn.
Each parish is offering prayers
It surely shows that everyone cares.
The doctor's orders he must abide
While droves of people flock to his bedside.
The Pope is supposed to rest and stay in bed
While he is intravenously fed.
Yet on Sunday during the Angelus
He went to the window and did surprise us.
He claims he'll be back soon
For his absence is causing economic doom.
His Holiness should return by Good Friday
For this expectation the throngs do pray.

Age 48
March 2005

My Freedom, "My" Kingdom

I desperately need my freedom
I want to control "My" Kingdom.
My home life is all but hell
And I am getting sicker, not well.
My head turns, my stomach aches
And I never get any breaks.
My life is anything but serene
And it's truly far from the life of a queen.
Queen Sofia of Spain, I am not
Yet I feel like a piece of snot.
Parents and bosses alike always yell
So I might as well crawl back into my shell.

Age 48
March 2005

A Visit to the Hospital

I came to the hospital to get some peace
Yet the woman's screams wouldn't cease.
I came here with a STRESS WHEEL
Creating it was no big deal.
I explained the percentage of my stress
And why my life is such a mess.
It was St. Pat's Day without the corned beef
Which gave me a bit of grief.
"The Apprentice" recap was a bore.
I was hoping for a whole lot more.
Her screams continued into the night
I'd like to tell her to "Go fly a kite."
Day one sure had its fill
As I tried to remain calm and still.
Finally, I watched the news
After sharing my soul and pouring the blues.

Age 48
March 2005

Hospital Visit, Part 2

Today Friday, people see me more at ease
I was happy and did as I pleased.
I slept late, then had breakfast
I used a pass and learned the hospital is vast.
Dr. Pilar came and visited me
I told her "I just want to be free."
I retrieved my calls on my breaks
While trying hard not to make mistakes.
During exercise class, I chose to dance
I was asserting myself and took a stance.
Later on I ate my lunch from home
As my mind continues to roam.
After lunch, there was occupational therapy
This to me is just fine and dandy.
I chose to paint a picture of a cat
For good, sound artistry is where I'm at.
Later in the afternoon, I changed my room
As I ponder a future full of doom.
Finally, I retired to my room, listened to the radio
After three trips down to the side patio.

Age 48
March 2005

The Beach Boys

The Beach Boys' concert came at last
And they truly gave us a blast!
The theater was packed & standing room only.
I danced, had fun & didn't feel lonely.

They sang "Sun, Sun, Sun"
While I had fun, fun, fun.
We danced & sang in the aisle
Though I needed a break after awhile.

I also heard "California Girls"
With all their tans & curls.
At one point, some of us ran toward the stage.
We looked like lions stampeding out of a cage.

Then there was "Lil' Ole Lady from Pasadena."
I bet her screams were like a hyena.
They continued as we jumped up & down
Yet no-one was wearing a frown.

Strangely, they didn't seem to mind
In fact, they treated us rather kind.
They shook hands, invited some up
After this, I felt like a full-bloomed buttercup.

Age 48
March 2005

The Ailing Pope

The "Holy Father" is getting worse
So all I want to do is curse.
He is getting very bad
And all Christians are very sad.
His reign has been long, far from brief
But now with his illness, we are full of grief.
Now he needs a tube to breathe
As I sit here, stew and seethe.
What has become of this great man
Who reached out to every person of every clan?
He's had the wisdom of King Solomon
And has proved to be intelligent, not dumb.
Unfortunately, the end is near, I'm sure
How much more can John Paul endure?
God has given him a heavy cross
And his death will be our loss.
I'm sure Our Pontiff will go to Heaven
After a life of serving His brethren.

Age 48
March 2005

The Setting Sun

The Sun was setting on the horizon
It was the end of a beautiful day.
Spring hath sprung at last
Soon the clocks will go back the other way.

It was such a pretty drive on the highway
Onward looking, the sky was brushed pink.
There were still interspersed patches of snow
Yet it is no longer time to wear mink.

It's 6:30 and it is still light
The days are growing a bit longer.
With April approaching
The sun's rays are getting stronger.

Age 48
March 2005

John Paul's Death

The "Holy Father" passed on today
So us Christians went to pray
While the weather was cloudy & gray.

The gray skies turned to teardrops of rain
Showing us the angels were in pain
On the departure of John Paul's reign.

He led a life that was oh, so humble
And speaking foreign tongues, he didn't fumble
With all of life's stress, he never did crumble.

He embraced all peoples, all nations
From Americans, Africans to Haitians
Making all visits pastoral vacations.

He kissed each nation on bended knee
Greeted everyone with face full of glee
For he wanted everyone to be free.

He held numerous rallies with youth
And he revived the Church's truth
While reading from the Book of Ruth.

Age 48
April 2005

He elevated many a hero
He prayed down at Ground Zero
He was beloved; far from Nero.

John Paul met with and revered Mother Teresa
While traveling, he never needed a visa
And always celebrated "Santa Misa."

He'll be known as the "People's Pope"
Who always s offered us so much hope
And finally showed us how to cope.

John Paul II travelled many a mile
Always wearing a beautiful smile
And he departed us with grace & style.

He's being nichnamed "John Paul the Great"
For he was full of love, not hate
And so, now he hath entered St. Peter's Gate.

Age 48
April 2, 2005

The Conclave Gets Ready

I wonder "Who's next"
To fill our void.
Who can replace John Paul
Whom most of us enjoyed?

The bookies' windows are open
They are strangely taking bets;
As the Vatican is preparing
And the conclave gets set.

Some say, Italy's Tetramazzi,
Others say, Germany's Ratzinger.
I just hope the voting is quick
And that the Conclave won't linger.

If no Pope is chosen,
The smoke will be black.
So the flock will wonder
"Who'll pick up the slack"?

When one is finally selected,
The smoke will be white.
The bells will also toll
To everyone's delight.

Age 48
April 2005

John Paul's Legacy

A saintly, frail man
Yet, oh so human.
Thus was John Paul II
Who loved Christian or Jew.
He was a true sign of hope
Over the years, showed us how to cope.

He's John Paul the Great
Now passing through St. Peter's Gate.

His faith and life were far from hollow
So he'll be a tough act to follow.
He's had many saintly traits
Therefore, his funeral was very ornate.
There've been screams of "Santo Subito"
For John Paul was never "Incognito."

He's John Paul the Great
Now passing through St. Peter's Gate.

He met the young, then the old
Essentially, he had a heart of gold.
The last few years were his Calvary
Yet he never ceased to pray to Mary.
Although he is gone,
His legacy will carry on.

He's John Paul the Great
Now passing through St. Peter's Gate!

Age 48
April 2005

Sadness in Rome

It's been raining a lot in Rome
Ever since the Pope is gone, not home.
Well, his new home is in Heaven
Where he's watching over His brethren.

I think the rain is a sign
A signal that we pine.
The rain equals our tears
And our new-found fears.

Fears of what lie ahead
An uneasy future that we dread.
Now the Cardinals are called to search
For a new leader of the Catholic Church.

It's called the "Conclave"
For they must be brave.
They'll lead a life of decency
While taking a strict vow of secrecy.

Age 48
April 2005

Knock-Knock-Knocking

I'm knock, knock-knocking on heaven's door
But I really don't know just want for.

I knock because I'm a lonely human
No-one listens yet anyone certainly can.

I knock to have a friend or two
Or even better to have a few.

I knock searching for my cupid
Because I Ain't that stupid.

I knock for approval and for love
Yet is God listening from above?

I knock at times for God to hear me
But does he really have eyes to see?

I knock and knock all day and all night
Yet no-one hears me or comes into sight.

I knock when I'm angry and upset
But my needs still AREN'T MET.

I knock 'cause I wanna be free
I knock 'cause I wanna be me.

Age 49
May 2005

Bergen Regional

Bergen Regional is not the hospital for me
There are too many crazies here you see.
Some get lucky, escape and flee
Yet all I want in life is to be free.

Some people scream and cuss and shout
While I get angry and hence I pout.
This is a hellhole without a doubt
And it sure takes time to get out.

At times, someone goes in the quiet room
It's empty and full of gloom and doom.
It's for the bad witch flying off her broom
While the rest are enjoying nature in full bloom.

At Bergen Regional one can't smoke
Privileges are gone, you might as well croak.
They take your money, and you go broke.
Being here is simply no joke.

Every pill you swallow is in the chart
Some of the staff are cold and have no heart.
It's also best to keep Dr. Rugalo and me far apart
For we are like whiskey and tonic-very tart.

One of the staff is a real prude
She checks everything, even your good.
God forbid if your actions are lewd
And if your behavior is rude.

Everything you do and say is in the book
And they give you that long, hard look.
Most treat you as if you were a crook
Only a few staff help to get you off the hook.

Finally, this hospital shouldn't be on the map
Points go against you if you take a nap.
The hospital food tastes like crap
That I don't even want it on my lap.

Age 49
May 2005

Silly Love

Why is that silly love
Coming down from above.
Yet found in a golden glove?

Do I have a hunch
That they will kick & punch
During a Monday Lunch?

It's better not to kill
Though love is all uphill
And yes, this is God's will.

Age 49
June 2005

John Paul Remembered

Pope John Paul
A pope for us all!
First kissing a baby
And doing it with glee.
Marrying a couple in love
Two fit like a glove.
Travelling the world around
Kneeling to kiss each ground.
Riding in an open Popemobile
Which was no big deal.
Trusting & loving everyone
Whether in the rain or in the sun.
John Paul—We sure miss you
For people like you are few.
An extraordinary friend
Til the very end.

Age 49
June 2005

A Lost Crane

A man spotted a strange crane
Perhaps his name is Wayne or Dwayne.
He has a large wing span
And runs faster than a man.
He was supposed to be miles away
But off his course he did not stray.
He's strayed from the Midwest
As he put onlookers to the test
And to naturalists he's become a guest.
From many a source I have heard
That this is really a unique bird.
He truly is a rare find
And a breed of a different kind.

Age 49
June 2005

Iraqi Elections

September two thousand three
Less and less people are free.
All over the world, there's fear & dread
Leading up to war and a lot dead.
It's now time for Iraqi elections
While the voters choose their selections.
Daily bombings happening all around
From the highest heights to the ground.
Insurgents trying to instill fear
While the second set of voters draws near.
No more Saddam or Al Qaeda, just ordinary folk
For the people of Iraq have finally spoke.

Age 49
June 2005

I Don't Belong

I Don't Belong
We don't get along
I no longer sing a song.

Can't you just see
That I wanna' be free
Why did God make me?

Why do I needlessly suffer-
When ma is so much tougher
And life gets rougher?

We yell & fight
Each & every night
For I want my rights.

Age 49
June 2005

God & His Plan

God made the world in Three
Heaven, earth and Hell you see.
We were made from the middle of the earth
For this is where we celebrate our birth.

After that we can achieve a place in heaven
Don't commit the deadly sins which are seven.
Or we shall eternally burn in Hell
Which would be like an infinity in a jail cell.

So pray that each day you do good
Just as you know that you should.
For in helping on earth, you'll gain grace
And soon you'll encounter God face to face.

Once again I implore, stay away from evil
For don't we already live in an upheaval?
Get out of harm's way if you must
Trust in God alone. Just Trust.

Age 49
June 2005

Kingdom Of Castles

There was a place with many a castle
Inhabitants lived there with hardly any hassle.
This renown place is Spain
With planted flowers on each window pane.
Life was a dream beyond compare
Work was plentiful and poverty was rare.
They were paid with the monetary unit-Peseta
In this rich land of the evergreen Meseta.
The most placid time was a century ago
With Valencia & Alicante using ports for cargo.
The better job was being a Knight in Shining Armor
While at the other end, was the poor, lonely farmer.
The most famous was probably El Cid
Fighting the Giants, eh the windmills, is what he did.
He fought in the area of "La Mancha"
It was so arid & dry you couldn't find a concha.
Sancho Panza, the squire, was a realist
And sadly to say Don Quijote was an idealist.

Age 49
June 2005

We're Gonna

We're gonna rock
And we're gonna' roll-
We'll take a vote
Down at the poll;
Then we'll meander
And take a stroll-
Over to the store
To buy a fur or stole.

We will walk
On another day-
Down to the beach
Or possibly the bay;
We'll sit & watch
The gorgeous Blue Jay
In the beautiful month
The month of May.

We're gonna' sing
And then dance-
With all our joy
Others we'll enhance;
We'll spend some money
And take a chance-
Perhaps we'll win
A trip to France.

We're gonna' kneel
At the altar-
And the priest will read
From the Holy Psaltar;
We'll take our vows
And we won't falter
With the maid-of-honor
In her pretty halter.

Age 49
June 2005

Nature

Bright amber was the sun
Yet it was seen by none.
Majestic blue was the sky
As the birds flew high.
Puffs of clouds brought us night
As the heavenly stars came into sight.
It's so beautiful how nature exists
But so sad to see how man resists.
We fight and tear each other apart
It's been like this from the start.
With daily killings, wars & foes
Then too are the various economic woes.
For Peace and Serenity will come to mind
When will act like the real human kind.

Age 49
July 2005

Summer of 2005

This summer by far, has been the worst
I swear by the devil, we've been cursed!
People are dizzy & slower yet still stoic
While the police & firefighters are heroic.
A scoop of ice cream takes 2-3 seconds to melt
While perspiration is the only thing I've felt.
I'm sure a cracked egg will fry on the sidewalk
This weather isn't fit for man, beast, or even a hawk.
This is even too hot for an Irish Setter
And I've finally done away with my sweater.
More is to come, I dismally hear
It's mid summer so I know autumn is near.
It can't come too soon, for we are in a bind
Too much more of this will make us go out of our minds.

Age 49
July 2005

God's Hand at Night

Today, July 29[h], the sunset was a beautiful sight
To many it was a midsummer's delight.
The horizontal sun was amber, hot & bright
It's another testimony to God's powerful might.

It shown so bright we were almost dazed
While in the midst of a summer all ablaze.
Sometimes it's hot, sometimes there's a haze
Not only here but where flocks graze.

It's so hot, we're sweaty & we drip
That women's hair is pulled back with a clip.
Oh please give me something, even a sip
And you, the weatherman, can you give us a tip?

Age 49
Aug. 2005

Asking Forgiveness

Frank—I know it was not right
That is seemed like I flew out of sight.
I waited and waited for over fifteen
And then my screaming, "Caused a scene."
I wanted to say "Thanks & also Goodbye"
Then the time on my watch surely did fly.
I really had to head back home
Back to the nest on my 4th Street home.
Again I plead don't be mad at me
For I really had to get going, you see.
Don't worry, I do have your umbrella
I'm no THIEF, just another "Good Fella."
And lastly don't forget soon I'll be Fifty
And I hope my day will be Nifty.

Age 49
June 2006

Mid July/Not Going

Not going into NYC
Is getting to be quite a pity.
Not going to Chelsea or downtown
Is making me wear a "Big Frown"!

It is a shame that all this "TERROR"
Is bringing on so much "HORROR"

Not going casually down Main Street
Is certainly no longer neat.
Not going to stroll down the Avenue
Is making be very, very Blue.

It is a shame that all this "TERROR"
Is bringing on so much "HORROR."

Not going from here to there
Is making me sit, pout and stare.
Not going calmly in a subway or bus
Is causing me grief and a lot of fuss.

It is a shame that all this "TERROR"
Is bringing on so much "HORROR."

Age 50
July 2006

Deadly Heat

Two days of oppressive Sub-Sahara heat
Have gotten most of the tri-state residents beat.

Ambulances stand ready and on call
While some people seek relief at their nearest mall.

Thunder and lightening have passed from sky to ground
As power outages happen all around.

Some Long Islanders haven't had power in over a week
And the near future continues to be bleak.

They are entering week 2 without electricity
Causing severe limitations to work and activity.

Lots of food is rotten, spoiled and bad
So when relief comes, people will be glad.

The very end of the month wasn't better
And no one even dared to wear a sweater.

The forecasters see no end to the heat wave
And all we can do is sweat, rant and rave.

Age 50
July 2006

Thank You Lord, Gracias, Senor

Thank you Lord for the lovely sunset
And thank you for the the new friend I met.
Gracias Senor para hacer la lilaca, el flor
Y gracias para violeta, el color.
Thank you Lord for being able to gamble with a quarter
And thank you for both tap and spring water.
Gracias Senor para darnos(la fiesta) de Pascua, un gran dia
Y gracias para darnos la libertad de celebrar alegria.
Thank you Lord for animals, especially dogs and cats
And thank you for the various types of winter hats.
Gracias Senor para tener noches con un bien sueno
Y gracias Senor para ser mi gran dueno.
Thank you Lord for the opportunity to serve the poor in a shelter
Thank you Lord whether it be in winter or a summer swelter.
Gracias Senor para hacer Navidad la major fiesta
Y gracias para hacer la nacion Espana con siesta.
Thank you Lord for watching us and being our Good Shepherd
And thank you for giving us the Holy Bible, your Word.
Gracias Senor para hacer la Sierra Madre
Y gracias para ser Nuestro Padre.
Thank you Lord for the creation of the bath tub
And thank you Lord for the soft scrubby to rub and rub.
Gracias Senor para todo que tengamos en el mundo
Y gracias gracias para esta tierra que se hizo y fundo.

Age 50
July 2006

My Dad

Why are you so nice
When some can be cold like ice?
Why are you so tolerant
When I can be very defiant ?
Why do you look to help everyone
When so many wrongs have been done?
Why is your outlook always positive
When others can be so negative?
Why do you always give me money
When I'm certainly no honey?
Why do you give twenty or forty
When I can be so naughty?

Dear Dad I love you
For all that you do.

Age 50
August 2006

The Shelter

St. Cecilia's Shelter is the place to be
For it's all about helping the poor you see
And when it is my turn, I am very happy.

It does not matter what color they are
Or if they came from close by or afar
Each is God's creation: a twinkling star.

They are chosen by need, not by looks
While each night they have hosts and cooks
And the shelter even provides an array of books.

After helping here, in this facility
No matter your capacity or ability
You leave with a bit more humility.

Age 50
August 2006

In Memoriam, Tessie Tortore

I mourn but I do not know why
I silently sigh, weep, and cry.
It is now August the sixth
And grandma's death is no myth.
I think of her often, oh so often
Yet my emotions harden and never soften.
As I write, her anniversary will approach
But who do I blame, who do I reproach?
Poor Grandma, Tess, died four years ago
And I feel her coffin was a piece of cargo.
But wait, wait—She was a such a lovely person
Very outgoing, lively witty, and so much fun.
I'm sure you made it thru Heaven's Gate
Where God and the Angles always wait.

Tessie Tortore 12/31/1907
8/17/2002

Age 50
August 2006

Dear Nuni

I had a dream about you today
That you were sick and on your way.
I guess I think of you often
And how you made hard times soften.
In the dream I had a job teaching
To the minds of children I was reaching.
The Sister came to get me
And then the crying started, you see.
If I only could be with you
For the world is fake, yet you were true.
I want to be where you are
Which from earth is very very far.
I'm sure you see the mess Bush made
Someone should spray him with Raid.
I really hope to join your someday
And let's fly in Heaven each and every day.

Age 50
August 2006

All I Want

All I want is peace
And for these absurd wars to cease.
I want joy, laughter, and riches
And jokes to put people in stitches.
I particularly want to see happiness
And lots of cures for sickness.
I'd like to see everyone with a pet dog or cat
And girls own dolls, boy with bats.
I'd like everyone to live in harmony
Whether they be ivory or ebony.
All I want are normal things
Like when the phone rings or a bird sings.

Age 50
August 2006

I Cannot Sleep

I cannot sleep.
My thoughts run deep.
At times I want to cry.
And run away and die.
Yet I don't seem to relax.
My mind is an automatic fax.
Perhaps I should run and hide.
But in whom would I confide?
My nerves are always on edge.
So only in God do I pledge?

Age 50
August 2006

If You're Here

If you're in Havana
You ought to eat a banana.
If you're at the beach
Why don't you buy a peach?
If you're at the Cape
Try a Concord grape.
If you're near the Fijis
Indulge with kiwis.
If you're on the ferry
Enjoy a juicy strawberry.
If you're on the Isle of Java
Bite into a Guava.
If you go to the moon
Don't forget a prune.
If you climb St. Helens
Eat some cool watermelon.
If you're at the state fair
Eat a bosc pear.
If you're at the Cape of Good Hope
Bring along a cantaloupe.
If you engage with the Sioux
Don't forget the honeydew.
If you're going to Yemen
Always pack a lemon.
If you visit a Catholic chapel
Don't forget about the forbidden apple.

Age 50
August 2006

A Trip To Hunter Mountain

A trip to Hunter Mountain
Only lacking a pretty fountain.
The August day was oh so fair
With crisp, fresh, incandescent air.
Hours filled with music, dancers and joy
And Children playing with their favorite toy.
Many types of jewelry and clothing vendors
With people spending lots of legal tender.
Later the sky was painted oh so bright
Made to the demand of God's delight.

Age 50
August 2006

President Bush

President Bush is a real pain
His horrible deeds leave a stain.
All he thinks about is war
Where the bloody carnage turns raw.
First he went into Afghanistan
Then Iraq & next will be Iran.
He ought to worry about the home front
Instead of looking for his next hunt.
We have health care problems and a botched system
It's darn well time I have voted for a Democrat.
Another mess is Social Security
And yet another is Medicare "D".
Wake Up! The war is unpopular and unjust
I can't wait to see your hearst.
There's a movie out "Death of a President"
Take heed, take heed, it's time you went.

Age 50
Sept. 2006

My 2006 Fall Trip

A tinge of yellow, a hue of red
Brisk, crisp mornings arising from bed.
A beautiful fall morn without a cloud
Fully enjoying this 'Time to Travel' crowd.
A lovely scenic route up to New England
With everyone lending a helping hand.
Our final destination will be Cape Cod
With our great driver, Fran, and of course God.
After a long ride, it'll be time to relax
Time to settle in before we spend the max.
I'll probably watch the Yankees & sew
Because tomorrow we'll really be on the go.
We have to arise and eat by seven
Oh, how I wish we'd leave by eleven!
Wednesday we are off on a Ferry Ride
With all of our cares & worries pushed aside.
Then we're off to a scrumptious lobster dinner
Oh gees how I wish I were a bit thinner.
However, I decided to have the salmon
While we ate, background music was a jammin'.
We sure were full when we were done
And Thursday we'll again be on the run.
Thursday we arose & went to the tip of the Cape
Still wishing I were in a lot better shape!
The day was sort of chilly & rather raw
As we listened about early commonwealth law.
Our guide Tom, shared a lot of history
Which too me seemed to be quite a mystery.
Fran drove all around, up and down
Than we made our way to Provincetown.

We looked at some famous lighthouses
And afterwards got sweats instead of blouses.
We all stopped to take a group photo
While Tom spoke about the Vikings and not Desoto.
We returned to the hotel after a hectic day
Only to learn we'd be going to a buffet.
The entertainment theme was "At the Hop."
With oldie favorites that were always on top.
For me the night ended all too soon
Because I was just beginning to croon.
On Friday we went to Foxwoods for awhile
And after winning I left with a smile.
I played poker and got a Royal Flush
Upon which I had an adrenaline rush.
At one, we decided to stop and eat
Being Friday, I had pasta but no meat.
We left by four and hit the road
Heading for home, where we'll unload.
Fran drove and then took ninety-five
Through Friday night traffic, she had to drive.
We were supposed to be home by eight
But got back at 10:00 which was very late.
For some the slow ride took its toll
Yet getting home safely was our main goal.
But essentially a great time was had by all
Going up to Cape Cod this 2006 fall.

Age 50
October 2006

The HIP Party

My HIP party of 2006 had entertainment
And after awhile it lead to sentiment.
I got up and took a chance
With great music I had to dance.
Someone had to get the ball rolling
And this was as fun as bowling.
After dancing solo a member of the band
Came forward, bowed and took my hand.
He told me that his name was Bill
And dancing with him was a thrill.
I asked the band to play the "Twist,"
At the end Bill turned me under his wrist.
Than Bill decided to do a slow fox trot
Yet when I was done I was hot.
The floor cleared, it was just Bill and me
My worries pushed aside I was so carefree.
As I headed for the bus he gave me a kiss
I went over the top & into a state of bliss.
A great time was had by all
During this memorable night in the fall.

Age 50
November 2006

Christmas 2006

This 2006 Christmas vacation
Was spent far away in Spain.
It was cold but no anticipation
Of having any rain.

First I went to Madrid
Land of the Meseta.
I did not go to see El Cid
And there's no more Peseta.

I finished my cat tapestry
And then bought another.
I'm using my money modestly
With permission of my mother.

From Madrid I visited a family
They live in Cuenca-un pueblo.
I ate without getting a homily
Than chatted with Paco, "mi abuelo."

From Cuenca I went to Granada
It was for rest & relaxation.
Cause I was tired or "cansada."
After the Christmas Celebration.

After the New Years embrace
I'll be back in Madrid.
I'll be arranging my suitcase
And telling others what I did.

Age 50
December 2006

Navidad 2006

Este ano gaste mi Navidad
Lejisimo en Espana, mi sueno.
Estaba gozando la hospitalidad
De Lucia y Paco, su dueno.

Despues de irme a Madrid
Me fue a visitor Cuenca, el pueblo.
No tenia ilusiones del Cid
Pero de celebrar con Paco, como mi abuelo.

Navidad fue una gran fiesta
Y despues de hacer mucho.
No tenia tiempo para la siesta
Ademas que bien fue el muchacho.

Luca decidio hacer mi ropa
Que bien de ella.
Durante los dias no come sopa
Pero decide comer paella.

Depues cinco dias
Yo me fue a Granada.
Pero en estos dias frias
No podia gozar una granizada.

Age 50
December 2006

A Late Storm

There's snow, snow, snow
So let's go, go, go.
I don't know when or where
But not here, over there.

Before going to the mall
Lets' make a snowball.
We can throw it up high
High towards the sky.

Then we can watch it drop
And it will suddenly stop.
Then we'll make a mad dash
To eat some cooked hash.

Age 50
December 2006

Our Discoverer

Christopher Columbus sailed the ocean blue
Because he had nothing else to do!
He sailed with three ships
And coincidentially made three trips!
First he discovered Haiti
With his girlfriend Katie.
Then he landed in Cuba
Where he learned to Scuba.
Finally, he came upon America
With the help of Isabel & not Erica.

Age 50
December 2006

A Prayer of Thanks

Thank you Lord for making me,
Thank you for letting me see Thee.
Thank you Lord for my gift of poetry,
And thank you for the art of embroidery.

Thank you Lord for giving us pets,
Thank you for both the Yanks and the Mets.
Thank you Lord for keeping me out of debts,
And thank you for flying me safely in jets.

Thank you Lord for your presence in the Chapel,
And thank you for making both Coke and Snapple.
Thank you for the delicious taste of an apple,
And thank you for the kiwi and pineapple.

Thank you Lord for the many miles I've flown,
For seeing things such as a rare bird or simple cone.
Thank you for knowing that I'm not alone,
On this lovely retreat called "Cornerstone."

Age 50
January 2007

Spring Is Near

The robin red breast are out
It's spring; so let us sing & shout.
The sky is crystal blue this day
With its hue, the sun is casting its ray.
Gone are the dank days; winter's past
And spring is finally here at last.
Gorgeous days are ahead
As sleepy heads arise from bed.
Children and adults will take to the outdoors
While shoppers flood the local stores.
Bright colored shorts will replace slacks
As men carry their jackets over their backs.
Squirrels are chasing each other here & there
Pretty soon it will be time for the spring fair.
So as you hear the birds chirp and sing
Just know this is a sure sign of spring!

Age 50
March 2007

Pilgrimage to Lourdes & Spain

Travelling through such rich green pastures
Made by the hands of the Master.
We had a lovely group dinner
And I'm still not going to get thinner.
Our first night we had a candlelight procession
Just a week after our Lord's Ascension.
On day two we had a town tour
And we went through many a door.
We visited Bernadette's house
Then in church, we were hushed like a mouse.
Frank & I had a lunch near the river
We had omelets & salami, but no liver.
Late PM on day two we had a Mass
And later still we passed a store of Swarwoski Crystal glass.
I was tempted, but I did not buy
For I'm off to Spain so I won't cry.
The next day travelling was uneventful
Just a very long day & pretty dull.
We went to Saragosa to pray
Yet still travelled much of the day.
Then we settled into our hotel for some sleep
After some embroidery into bed did I creep.
Day five found us going to Montserret
In the motor coach, again we sat.
This time we stayed for two nights
And this sure took us to new heights.
The mountains there are very, very tall
And in Montserrat the Benedictines call.

Later on we took a side trip to Barcelona
A long, long distance from Verona.
After a tedious day we went to bed
Pondering all the things that were said.
Valencia would be our last stop
Where there's good weather for many a crop.
Here again we spent two nights
Just enough to take in the sights.
We're on a trip to visit the Holy Grail
And bid Spain "adios" before we set sail.
During the night there was a horrible storm
And in Spain this is not the norm.
One lady, Shirley, celebrated her birthday
So I went all out in a unique way.
I got her a special Spanish Cake
Which the 'Corte Ingles' did bake.
It's this country, Spain, I've come to love
Made from the Master from above.

Age 50
May 22-30 2007

The Summer Birds

The first morning of summer
I heard a lot of birds.
They were chirping and cooing
And singing a lot of words.

Dad told us that the mother
Was perched up on her nest.
He told us it was a dove
And not a robin red-breast.

He also explained to us
That the nest was on top of our home.
After laying an egg or two
The mom will stay near and won't roam.

If she does fly away
It's a quick trip for food.
She has to gather worms or grass
To nourish her new brood.

After a very early feeding
Its' time for a nap.
The chirping and cooing die down
As the corner of my house is a earthly map.

By 6AM, all was quiet and calm
And I didn't hear a peep.
I softened the background music
And tried to drift off to sleep.

Age 52
June 2008

The Demise of Human Civilization

Human Civilization has gone crazy
Some people are mad and others lazy.
And still others completely amaze me.

In some ways, we've gone back to being prehistoric
Perhaps even being a bit animalistic
And by no means are we moralistic.

I'm beginning to think respect is in my dreams
For people today no longer know what courtesy means
And can't you hear all silent screams?

People congregate, stand still and won't move
For no-one seems to be in a happy groove
And what does it all prove?

People are in a rush, then push and shove
So I look up to God above
And ask Him, "What ever happened to love?"

You can say "Excuse me" til you're blue in the face
Yet everyone seems to be in the same rat race
And why do I need a poem to state my case?

Age 52
July 2008

Headaches and An MRI

I have a lot of headaches
And they are real, not fakes
And I feel like I'm at my wake.

So I want to cry
But I don't want to die
For I need an MRI.

On the cot I need to lie still
In a room that has a chill
Hopefully, I won't have a hefty bill.

I hope its just a rumor
That I think I have a brain tumor
And I lack a sense of humor.

Age 52
July 2008

My friend Jeanne

My friend is a true royal queen
If you know what I mean
And her name is Jean.

A smile is always in place
On her cute, pretty face
And she's never in a rat-race.

My friend Jeanne is so unique
In my mind she's chic
And she's so humble and meek.

Jeanne treats you like no one would
For she is so very good
That she does everything she could.

She truly has a heart of gold
For being only 43 years old
And she comes from a special mold.

Age 52
July 20008

Doctors

Doctors are one group that I can't stand
For their attitudes, are anything but bland.
They make you wait (in the room) way too long
And as for me, everything they do is wrong.
They give you a lot of unneeded tension
By asking every type of silly, dopey question.
They really don't care if you're the one they hurt
And most doctors are unpleasant, yet curt.
They love to jab & stick you with needles
Especially if you're old, handicapped or feeble.
You're damned if you do and damned if you don't
Oh go back to certain Doctors—I won't, I won't, I won't.
But if I have to, I get nervous and throw up
Oh heck-I'd rather turn into a small pup.

Age 52
Sept. 2008

Headaches

Headaches can be a royal pain
Especially if you get a migraine.
They usually come and go at will
And they leave after a strong pill.
Some of them come from stress
And mine are coming in excess.
Caffeine can probably trigger them the worst
That at times you feel that you have been cursed.
Another trigger can be a strong light
Especially those that are strobe or bright.
At times my head is full and very busy
The effect is becoming nauseas and dizzy.
When I get a headache I know I'm cursed
By my those migraines are the worst.

Age 52
November 2008

Wide Awake!

Oh Gosh! I'm wide awake
It's only four and not even eight.
I really don't feel good
Not like I ought to or should.
Now, I ask does anyone care-
I guess not, for nobody seems to stare.
Oh, in my stomach I have sharp pangs
At least I'm not dreaming of hostile gangs.
I don't sleep well after watching the news.
Who does, after hearing the nations' blues?
There are fires, floods and other bad things happening.
So all I do is say a prayer and end it with a simple. Amen.

Age 52
Nov. 2008

My friend Irene

I contacted a friend to tell her my good fortune
But what I told her was soon undone.
She began to tell me of her bad news
And she told me her story and sang the blues.
When I heard all this, I started to cry
As I paced the floor, I Pondered Why?
She was in an accident & lost her legs
My brain went numb & felt like frozen eggs.
Irene always wanted me to have a place of my own
But twenty years ago, I had a head like a stone.
I wouldn't listen to anything she had to say
For I always wanted it my own way.
Years ago she was always very good to me
And happiness has always been her key.

Age 52
December 2008

An Early Christmas Gift

I've been finding a lot of lucky pennies of late
And I bet this is changing my fate.
All good things are happening so very fast
And they are changing my ugly past.
For me, Christmas sure came early this year
And I have been shedding many a happy tear.
I am soon getting an apartment, you see
And now, I'm as busy as a bee.
Jeanne, my friend, is helping as much as she can
And soon we will be getting a moving van.
I have a new social worker named Eva
I bet she's as nice & pretty as a diva.
And Priscilla is the name of my agent
She sounds like she's been Heaven sent.
I am also getting my poetry published soon
Sometimes I feel like I am flying to the moon.
All my wishes are finally falling into place
And my life is doing an about face.
When excited, there are nights that I cannot sleep.
And in my mind, I am saying OBLEEP.
My thoughts are running wild
And I'm as giddy as a happy child.
God above has finally answered my prayers
And now I know he truly cares.
He has answered my prayers as He sees fit
And now my Eternal Light has been lit.

Age 52
December 2008

In Conclusion

I'm up there now and all poetried out
With nothing much left to write about.
I've written about Canada, Italy and Spain
And I even wrote a poem about weather and rain.
I covered all the types of money
As well as topics both sad and funny.
I covered both Vietman and the Iraqi war
And the current recession knocking at our door.
I wrote about Mother Teresa & Cardinal O'Connor
While trying to show their views regarding terror.
I included God's creation & wrote about my pet
And in retrospect, things I probably regret.
I wrote about St. John's—my church
And of a beautiful cardinal mounted on a perch.
I've written about my many trips and my recent cruise
I even wrote about various food and stews.
I've written a lot about Jeanne, my friend
And now I think I have come to my end.

Age 52
December

Edwards Brothers Malloy
Thorofare, NJ USA
September 17, 2013